Disaster Relief

Affirmative Action
Amateur Athletics
American Military Policy
Animal Rights
Capital Punishment
DNA Evidence
Educational Standards
Election Reform
The FCC and Regulating Indecency
Fetal Rights
Freedom of Speech
Gay Rights
Gun Control
Immigrants' Rights After 9/11
Immigration Policy
Legalizing Marijuana
Mandatory Military Service
Media Bias
Mental Health Reform
Miranda Rights
Open Government
Physician-Assisted Suicide
Policing the Internet
Prisoners' Rights
Private Property Rights
Protecting Ideas
Religion in Public Schools
The Right to Die
The Right to Privacy
Rights of Students
Search and Seizure
Smoking Bans
Stem Cell Research and Cloning
Tort Reform
Trial of Juveniles as Adults
The War on Terror
Welfare Reform
Women in the Military

Disaster Relief

Alan Marzilli

SERIES CONSULTING EDITOR
Alan Marzilli, M.A., J.D.

CHELSEA HOUSE
P U B L I S H E R S
An imprint of Infobase Publishing

363.3480973
M393d

Disaster Relief

Copyright © 2007 by Infobase Publishing

Chelsea House
An imprint of Infobase Publishing
132 West 31st Street
New York, NY 10001

Library of Congress Cataloging-in-Publication Data

Marzilli, Alan.
  Disaster relief / Alan Marzilli.
    p. cm. — (Point/counterpoint)
  Includes bibliographical references and index.
  ISBN-13: 978-0-7910-9554-6 (hardcover)
  ISBN-10: 0-7910-9554-1 (hardcover)
  1. Disaster relief—United States. 2. Assistance in emergencies—United States.
3. Disasters—United States. 4. United States. Federal Emergency Management
Agency. I. Title. II. Series.

  HV555.U6M364 2007
  363.34'80973—dc22   2007015481

Series design by Keith Trego
Cover design by Keith Trego and Joo Young An

Printed in the United States of America

Bang NMSG 10 9 8 7 6 5 4 3 2 1

This book is printed on acid-free paper.

1/09

CONTENTS

Foreword
Alan Marzilli, M.A., J.D.
Washington, D.C.

The debates presented in POINT/COUNTERPOINT are among the most interesting and controversial in contemporary American society, but studying them is more than an academic activity. They affect every citizen; they are the issues that today's leaders debate and tomorrow's will decide. The reader may one day play a central role in resolving them.

Why study both sides of the debate? It's possible that the reader will not yet have formed any opinion at all on the subject of this volume—but this is unlikely. It is more likely that the reader will already hold an opinion, probably a strong one, and very probably one formed without full exposure to the arguments of the other side. It is rare to hear an argument presented in a balanced way, and it is easy to form an opinion on too little information; these books will help to fill in the informational gaps that can never be avoided. More important, though, is the practical function of the series: Skillful argumentation requires a thorough knowledge of *both* sides—though there are seldom only two, and only by knowing what an opponent is likely to assert can one form an articulate response.

Perhaps more important is that listening to the other side sometimes helps one to see an opponent's arguments in a more human way. For example, Sister Helen Prejean, one of the nation's most visible opponents of capital punishment, has been deeply affected by her interactions with the families of murder victims. Seeing the families' grief and pain, she understands much better why people support the death penalty, and she is able to carry out her advocacy with a greater sensitivity to the needs and beliefs of those who do not agree with her. Her relativism, in turn, lends credibility to her work. Dismissing the other side of the argument as totally without merit can be too easy—it is far more useful to understand the nature of the controversy and the reasons *why* the issue defies resolution.

The most controversial issues of all are often those that center on a constitutional right. The Bill of Rights—the first ten amendments to the U.S. Constitution—spells out some of the most fundamental rights that distinguish the governmental system of the United States from those that allow fewer (or other) freedoms. But the sparsely worded document is open to interpretation, and clauses of only a few words are often at the heart of national debates. The Bill of Rights was meant to protect individual liberties; but the needs of some individuals clash with those of society as a whole, and when this happens someone has to decide where to draw the line. Thus the Constitution becomes a battleground between the rights of individuals to do as they please and the responsibility of the government to protect its citizens. The First Amendment's guarantee of "freedom of speech," for example, leads to a number of difficult questions. Some forms of expression, such as burning an American flag, lead to public outrage—but nevertheless are said to be protected by the First Amendment. Other types of expression that most people find objectionable, such as sexually explicit material involving children, are not protected because they are considered harmful. The question is not only where to draw the line, but how to do this without infringing on the personal liberties on which the United States was built.

The Bill of Rights raises many other questions about individual rights and the societal "good." Is a prayer before a high school football game an "establishment of religion" prohibited by the First Amendment? Does the Second Amendment's promise of "the right to bear arms" include concealed handguns? Is stopping and frisking someone standing on a corner known to be frequented by drug dealers a form of "unreasonable search and seizure" in violation of the Fourth Amendment? Although the nine-member U.S. Supreme Court has the ultimate authority in interpreting the Constitution, its answers do not always satisfy the public. When a group of nine people—sometimes by a five-to-four vote—makes a decision that affects the lives of hundreds of millions, public outcry can be expected. And the composition of the Court does change over time, so even a landmark decision is not guaranteed to stand forever. The limits of constitutional protection are always in flux.

These issues make headlines, divide courts, and decide elections. They are the questions most worthy of national debate, and this series aims to cover them as thoroughly as possible. Each volume sets out some of the key arguments surrounding a particular issue, even some views that most people consider extreme or radical—but presents a balanced perspective on the issue. Excerpts from the relevant laws and judicial opinions and references to central concepts, source material, and advocacy groups help the reader to explore the issues even further and to read "the letter of the law" just as the legislatures and the courts have established it.

It may seem that some debates—such as those over capital punishment and abortion, debates with a strong moral component—will never be resolved. But American history offers numerous examples of controversies that once seemed insurmountable but now are effectively settled, even if only on the surface. Abolitionists met with widespread resistance to their efforts to end slavery, and the controversy over that issue threatened to cleave the nation in two; but today public debate over the merits of slavery would be unthinkable, though racial inequalities still plague the nation. Similarly unthinkable at one time was suffrage for women and minorities, but this is now a matter of course. Distributing information about contraception once was a crime. Societies change, and attitudes change, and new questions of social justice are raised constantly while the old ones fade into irrelevancy.

Whatever the root of the controversy, the books in POINT/ COUNTERPOINT seek to explain to the reader the origins of the debate, the current state of the law, and the arguments on both sides. The goal of the series is to inform the reader about the issues facing not only American politicians, but all of the nation's citizens, and to encourage the reader to become more actively involved in resolving these debates, as a voter, a concerned citizen, a journalist, an activist, or an elected official. Democracy is based on education, and every voice counts—so every opinion must be an informed one.

This volume examines a controversy on the minds of most Americans in late summer of 2005, a controversy that remains important to a large area of the nation: disaster relief. Hurricane Katrina destroyed homes and businesses throughout Louisiana, Mississippi, and neighboring states and killed more than 1,000 people. News coverage focused not only on the destructive nature of the storm, but also on the plight of those trapped in its wake, waiting on rooftops or makeshift rafts to be rescued or crowded into a stadium with inadequate sanitary facilities. Local and state politicians gained national prominence as they pleaded for help, and viewers across the country wondered why we were not better prepared for a storm that had been tracked for many days before hitting the Gulf Coast. As the region continued to rebuild, politicians at all levels of government played the "blame game," but in fact politicians had debated for years about whether the federal government should be more active in preparing for and responding to natural disasters or the states and local governments should accept greater responsibility. In addition to that controversy, this volume examines disagreements over the adequacy of federal financial aid to disaster victims and the future of a federal program that provides low-cost flood insurance—a program that had to borrow more than $20 billion of taxpayers' money to pay out claims related to Hurricane Katrina and Hurricane Rita, which followed soon after.

When Disaster Strikes

Throughout the history of the United States, natural disasters have posed a risk to life and property. Early in the nation's history, before technological advances enhanced humans' ability to predict weather, build safer homes, and evacuate populations from harm's way, several notable disasters proved deadly. In 1900, a hurricane in Galveston, Texas, killed an estimated 8,000 people; the 1906 San Francisco earthquake killed about 3,000; and tornadoes in the Midwest killed nearly 700 on March 18, 1925.

Although Americans have devised strategies for reducing the number of deaths that cataclysmic events such as these could cause, natural disasters continue to have a strong economic impact and cause disruption to people's lives. As the U.S. population shifted south (particularly to Florida), more people moved to coastal areas, and beach houses became more extravagant, the economic impact of natural disasters became staggering. Starting

10

with Hurricane Hugo in 1989—the first U.S. disaster to top $1 billion in damages—a series of natural disasters has caused damages costing billions of dollars.

Hurricane Andrew struck the coast of Florida in 1992 as a Category 5 hurricane. (Hurricanes are ranked on a scale of 1 to 5, with 5 being the strongest.) Andrew damaged most of the roofs in Dade County, where Miami is located, and destroyed more than 100,000 homes. There were scattered incidents of looting, and many residents lost electricity or access to clean drinking water, prompting local officials to criticize the federal government for not responding quickly enough to appeals for help. All told, Hurricane Andrew caused more than $20 billion in damages. The Federal Emergency Management Agency (FEMA)— the federal agency with primary responsibility for responding to disasters—spent about $1.8 billion on the disaster.

Less than two years later, another major disaster struck the other side of the country. While most Californians were sleeping, the Northridge earthquake struck Los Angeles and the surrounding communities, killing 61 people, destroying about 60,000 houses and apartment units, and causing an estimated $40 billion in damages. FEMA spent nearly $7 billion on recovery efforts.

Although these disasters caused widespread damage and attracted national attention and activity from lawmakers, the 2005 hurricane season caught the nation completely off guard. In late August, as Category 5 Hurricane Katrina drove through the Gulf of Mexico, New Orleans mayor Ray Nagin ordered an evacuation of the city. Experts predicted a storm surge of water 28 feet high. New Orleans, a city surrounded by water and built below sea level, had levees (or flood walls) that were only capable of handling a 17-foot surge. Further complicating matters was the fact that some of the levees were beginning to fail.

As Katrina crashed ashore, it had dropped to Category 3 strength, but the real problem was the storm surge that it created. Levees collapsed, flooding large portions of the city. With thousands unable or unwilling to evacuate, the storm killed

This aerial photograph of downtown New Orleans shows rising flood waters threatening that entire portion of the city on September 1, 2005. In the middle is the Superdome, the sports stadium where many residents took refuge after being evacuated because of Hurricane Katrina.

more than 1,000 people, mostly in Louisiana and Mississippi. Some New Orleans residents drowned while attempting to escape the flood by taking refuge in their attics.

The nation watched in horror as the television networks showed nonstop aerial footage of Katrina's aftermath. Dead bodies floated in the water; cars and homes were washed away; thousands of evacuees were crowded into the Superdome sports stadium without adequate supplies or toilets; widespread looting was driven partially by the need for food, but looters also stole electronic equipment and other goods. Mayor Nagin and Louisiana Governor Kathleen Blanco became well-known figures as they pleaded with the nation for help, some of which came from the federal government, some of which came from private organizations like the Red Cross, and some of which came from volunteers across the nation. FEMA Director Michael Brown also became infamous. A former lawyer and horse show judge who had little emergency management experience, Brown was widely criticized for his handling of the disaster, leading to his resignation and, later, the reorganization of FEMA.

Before rebuilding of the damaged areas could get underway, Hurricane Rita struck the Gulf Coast, rubbing salt into the region's wounds. In both of these major natural disasters, the federal government played a major role in helping people rebuild their lives and homes. With Katrina and Rita, the federal government appropriated more than $50 billion in aid to the region affected by the storms. However, its involvement in disaster relief generates a great deal of controversy. Although many people are grateful for the federal aid and assistance, numerous critics believe that the federal government does not do enough for people in dire need in the wake of a disaster. With Hurricane Katrina, especially, the failure of the government to respond more quickly and in a more organized manner—complicated by the fact that many of the levees that failed were maintained by the U.S. Army Corps of Engineers—led to charges that the federal government does not do enough to protect its citizens from danger.

On the other hand, preparing for disasters, withstanding them, and rebuilding afterward are all extremely costly. Many people question whether the federal government—and by extension, taxpayers throughout the nation—should bear the financial responsibility for natural disasters. These critics argue that individuals should protect themselves financially by purchasing natural disaster insurance, and that local and state governments should do more to protect their citizens from the types of disasters that occur locally.

Components of Federal Disaster Relief

The federal government helps people withstand and recover from natural disasters in a number of ways. Some forms of assistance come before a disaster has occurred, such as mitigation (building structures to withstand disasters), planning, and insurance. Other forms of assistance are made available as a disaster approaches or as it hits, such as providing shelter and supplies, including food, water, and medical supplies. Finally, post-disaster relief helps people recover from the effects of a disaster. The Robert T. Stafford Disaster Relief and Emergency Assistance Act, generally

Senate Report Finds Failure at Local, State, and National Levels

A Senate investigation of the federal response to Katrina also examined the response of local and state governments. The report found that officials at each of these levels of government failed the people of the Gulf Coast:

…The suffering that continued in the days and weeks after the storm passed did not happen in a vacuum; instead, it continued longer than it should have because of—and was in some cases exacerbated by—the failure of government at all levels to plan, prepare for, and respond aggressively to the storm. These failures were not just conspicuous; they were pervasive. Among the many factors that contributed to these failures, the Committee found that there were four overarching ones: (1) long-term warnings went unheeded and government officials neglected their duties to prepare for a forewarned catastrophe; (2) government officials took insufficient actions or made poor decisions in the days immediately before and after landfall; (3) systems on which officials relied to support their response efforts failed; and (4) government officials at all levels failed to provide effective leadership. These individual failures, moreover, occurred against a backdrop of failure, over time, to develop the capacity for a coordinated, national response to a truly catastrophic event, whether caused by nature or man-made.

The results were tragic loss of life and human suffering on a massive scale, and an undermining of confidence in our governments' ability to plan, prepare for, and respond to national catastrophes.

Source: U.S. Senate Committee on Homeland Security and Governmental Affairs, *Hurricane Katrina: A Nation Still Unprepared* (May 2006), p. 2.

referred to as the Stafford Act, governs much of the federal disaster relief program.

One of the more visible forms of disaster mitigation by the federal government is the construction and maintenance of flood-control levees by the U.S. Army Corps of Engineers. Of course, the failure of the levees in New Orleans generated a great deal of attention, but the corps has created countless flood control projects that are now owned by local governments, and it continues to operate nearly 400 dams and reservoirs for flood control purposes. By the organization's own estimate, its flood control projects prevented more than $200 billion in damages between 1991 to 2000.

The federal government further encourages communities to reduce flood damage by limiting sales of federally backed flood insurance to communities that participate in floodplain management activities. FEMA cooperates with participating communities to create maps that show flood risks, and identify "special flood hazard areas" (SFHAs). The community must then require that all new buildings—or those that have been damaged or rebuilt—follow flood-proofing measures, which might include raising the elevation of a home on piers in coastal areas. For areas susceptible to hurricanes, the federal government also established the National Hurricane Program (NHP) in 1985. The program helps local communities to assess their risk of damages from wind and water, and to develop building codes that reflect hurricane risk.

Another example of disaster mitigation is the National Earthquake Hazards Reduction Program (NEHRP), which Congress established in 1977. A collaborative effort between FEMA and other federal agencies, NEHRP seeks to reduce earthquake destruction by improving scientists' ability to predict earthquakes; by developing model building codes with architectural measures that help buildings withstand earthquakes; by encouraging local and state governments to adopt these codes; and through educating the public about earthquake risks and how to minimize them.

The federal government also plays a role in disaster preparedness planning, from the national level all the way down to individual households. The NHP includes a training and planning component, helping communities prepare for hurricanes by training local officials and emergency responders, and working with communities to plan hurricane evacuation routes and procedures. To qualify for enhanced grant funding under the Stafford Act, local and state governments must participate in planning for disasters. Additionally, FEMA devotes resources to helping Americans prepare for disaster—for example, by publishing materials that educate people about what to do in case of a tornado warning.

Financially, the best way for people to prepare for a disaster is to make sure that they have the proper insurance. Many people pay for homeowner's insurance and renter's insurance, both of which provide reimbursement for damages to homes and personal belongings. Most insurance is purchased from private insurance companies, but many of them are not willing to provide insurance for disasters because of the risk that many homes will be damaged at the same time, leading to huge financial losses for the insurer. Throughout the nation, standard homeowners' policies exclude flood damage; however, in some places, insurance companies exclude disasters for which that location is particularly at risk, such as excluding earthquake damage in California or hurricane damage in Florida. State governments have responded by creating their own insurance programs for local risks, and the federal government currently sponsors the National Flood Insurance Program (NFIP). Many lawmakers have proposed support for a national program to provide insurance for all types of disasters.

Although some disasters, such as earthquakes, take everyone by surprise, other forms of natural disasters, such as tornadoes and hurricanes, can be predicted before they hit. With hurricanes especially, the federal response can begin before the damage begins. When a tropical storm threatens to cause damage in the United States, FEMA deploys its Hurricane Liaison

Team to the National Hurricane Center in Miami. The team communicates with state and local officials to provide detailed information about the storm's progress and likely effects and to coordinate the evacuation process if necessary.

After the disaster strikes, the federal government provides relief under the Stafford Act if, on the request of a state governor (or several states' governors), the president declares a federal disaster area. At first, the government provides emergency assistance, which can include supporting search and rescue missions; providing food, water, and medical supplies; and providing cash assistance to individuals and families for immediate needs, such as food, transportation, and temporary lodging.

On a longer-term basis, the federal government might provide assistance to families, such as trailer homes to live in while they rebuild their houses, and relief from taxes while they are displaced by the disaster. FEMA also provides money for the minimal repairs needed to make a home habitable again, but not necessarily for restoring it to its prior condition—in other words, bailing out the water and patching up the holes. Homeowners without sufficient insurance to rebuild can take out low-interest loans from the U.S. Small Business Administration (SBA), another way that the federal government supports disaster recovery.

A Brief History of Federal Disaster Relief

Flooding of the Mississippi River first motivated the federal government to respond to natural disasters. The response was initially dominated by federal support of the construction of levees. Flooding of the river in the 1850s through the 1870s led Congress to form the Mississippi River Commission in 1879. For nearly 50 years, the commission constructed levees to protect areas around the river from flooding. However, according to a Congressional Research Service Report:

> As the levee system neared completion in 1927, a massive
> flood overwhelmed the flood control project, damaging the

reputation of the commission. While the levee system failed, the commitment to solve the flood problem solidified. The Flood Control Act of 1936 launched a national program of structural flood control works. Together, the establishment of the commission in 1879 and the 1936 act highlighted a 60-plus year period when the federal government dealt with the threat of flooding in two basic ways: structural flood controls on rivers and shorelines (e.g., dams and levees), and post-disaster assistance for flood victims.[1]

In the 1950s, with private insurance companies increasingly unwilling to provide flood coverage, President Harry Truman attempted to form a national flood insurance program, and later Congress developed a similar program. The program never received funding, however, and was dissolved. After hurricanes and flooding caused widespread damage in the 1960s, Congress passed the National Flood Insurance Act of 1968, which established NFIP and institutionalized the process of mapping flood hazards.

Until the 1970s, financial assistance in the wake of disasters had taken place largely on an ad hoc (as needed) basis, starting with an act of Congress in 1803 that provided aid to a New Hampshire town badly damaged by fire. In 1974, Congress passed the Disaster Relief Act, which formalized the process by which the president declared disasters. Five years later, in 1979, President Jimmy Carter brought together the many federal disaster relief functions—more than 100 federal agencies had disaster response functions at the time—in forming FEMA.

Current Controversies

It is impossible to discuss federal disaster relief policy today without viewing it largely through the lens of the federal response to hurricanes Katrina and Rita. Not only were the disasters by far the most expensive natural disasters for the federal government to date, but a major city was virtually wiped out, and the storms caused extensive damage to an area larger than the United Kingdom. Perhaps more significant was the widespread television coverage of destruction and death. This, coupled with startling reports of FEMA's inefficient response to the hurricanes, led most Americans to believe that the federal disaster response system was deeply flawed.

Although disaster relief activities include responses to terrorists attacks (such as those of September 11, 2001), the failure of nuclear power plants, and various other human-made disasters, as well as responses to disasters overseas, this book is limited to an examination of the federal government's response to natural disasters, such as tornadoes, hurricanes, and earthquakes. As noted, much of the current debate is discussed in the context of hurricanes Katrina and Rita.

One area of the ongoing controversy is influenced by other political debates: to what extent should the federal government be involved in disaster relief? Although disaster relief is firmly rooted in laws such as the Stafford Act, recent years have seen increasing attacks on the size and spending habits of the federal government, coupled with increased support for states' rights. Supporters of federalism—a limited federal government with most responsibility for issues affecting individual states lying with the government of the states themselves. Many people blamed the government's inefficient response to Hurricane Katrina not on the people who led the response, but on the fact that the states are better positioned to respond to disasters than the federal government.

Many eyebrows have been raised over the amount of federal expenditures on disaster relief—more than $50 billion for hurricanes Katrina and Rita—as well as the method by which financial assistance has been distributed. Investigations into the ways in which FEMA spent money revealed very loose controls on how funds were spent—there were instances of prisoners receiving disaster relief checks and people using FEMA's money to purchase diamond jewelry. At the same time, many in the disaster-stricken Gulf Coast region have said that financial assistance has been insufficient to meet the needs of disaster victims, and a few high-profile stories of fraud and waste are detracting attention from the widespread needs that remain.

Many of Katrina's and Rita's victims would be better off financially if they had purchased flood insurance from NFIP; in fact, one of the goals of federal sponsorship of NFIP is to reduce post-disaster spending. Some people question whether offering financial assistance to those who do not have insurance sends the wrong message about personal responsibility. At the same time, enough people in the disaster area had flood insurance through NFIP that there were immense losses to the program. Payouts to victims of Katrina and Rita have totaled about $24 billion, compared to the $2 billion per year that the program brings in from policyholders' insurance premium payments. NFIP had to borrow money from the federal government, leaving taxpayers to foot the bill for much of the flood damage, despite the existence of the program. Further, many argue that making flood insurance available in flood-prone areas encourages people to make unwise decisions about where to build houses.

Summary

The federal government faced widespread criticism for its handling of hurricanes Katrina and Rita. Many said the government did not do enough to assist disaster victims, while others said that the government was too generous with taxpayers' money. Most people, however, agree that the federal government did not respond in an efficient manner to the disasters. Although FEMA underwent significant changes after the disaster, many issues remain contentious, including the relative role of state and federal governments, the generosity of federal financial assistance, and the continuation of the National Flood Insurance Program.

The Federal Government Should Play a Stronger Role in Disaster Preparedness and Relief

During natural disasters accompanied by widespread power outages, ice can be a lifesaver. In the absence of refrigeration, ice is needed to keep food and milk from spoiling and to store some medications, such as insulin for diabetics. In the aftermath of Hurricane Katrina, which left people throughout the Gulf Coast region without power, FEMA attempted to provide ice to hurricane victims. Due to mismanagement, however, less than half of the ice purchased by the federal government ever made it to hurricane victims, and the costs in purchasing, transporting, and storing the ice were many times what they should have been.

One of the enduring stories from the federal response to Katrina was that of an exasperated truck driver who donated a truckload of ice to the polar bears at the Reid Park Zoo in Tucson, Arizona, while thousands of residents in Gulf Coast states were stuck without electricity. His odyssey took him through 22 states, as he tried in vain to learn from FEMA officials where to take his ice. Finally, he decided that it would be better to give the polar bears some ice to enjoy than to continue driving around in frustration. FEMA officials directed other truckloads of ice around the country, with a Senate investigation revealing that:

> [s]ome of the ice ended up in Portland, Maine—1,600 miles from the disaster area. The cost of handling and storing the 200-plus truckloads of ice that went to Portland was approximately $275,000. More ice went to other distant locations around the country because FEMA decided it made more sense to move the ice to cold-storage facilities for use in new disasters than to let it melt. It is not clear that this was the most cost-effective choice, given the lack of planning that resulted in trucks being rerouted multiple times, and sometimes sitting idle for days, all while costs to the government were mounting.
>
> On September 16, NBC News reported that it had found trucks full of ice in locations such as Maryland, Missouri, Georgia, and Tennessee. Some of the trucks had been driving and/or sitting idle with their full loads for two weeks. One truck driver reported that he had begun his trip in Oshkosh, Wisconsin, traveled to Louisiana, then was sent to Georgia, but was rerouted to South Carolina, before being sent to Cumberland, Maryland. NBC News later reported that the truck was then sent to Iowa, where the ice was put into cold storage. The driver reported that this cost taxpayers at least an extra $9,000. When multiplied by hundreds of truckloads that also took circuitous routes to cold storage, the wasted taxpayer dollars begin to add up.[2]

Only the federal government has the resources necessary to respond to a large-scale disaster.

While debating an aid package of more than $50 billion, in addition to a multibillion-dollar aid package that had passed earlier, Representative Joseph Crowley of New York argued that the Katrina disaster was of such magnitude that Congress should have focused exclusively on Katrina relief until the Gulf Coast region recovered:

> Today's support is a strong step, but it [is] not the last step. The last time this many people were displaced was during the Civil War. This Congress must get back to work in a bi-partisan manner, and address the needs both immediate and future, of the victims of Hurricane Katrina. And we should not adjourn or recess until we do so. Tax-cuts, estate tax repeal, plans to privatize Social Security, should all take a back burner, while these people suffer.
>
> We must work to bring the full Federal resources of this government to help these people get back into their homes as quickly as possible, and to rebuild their lives.[3]

To Crowley, the duty of the federal government was not limited to basic recovery efforts, such as cleaning up flood debris and repairing levees. Rather, he argued that Katrina should serve as a national call to attention to the poverty in which many in the Gulf Coast region had been living prior to the hurricane. He maintained that the government had a duty to rebuild the region so that its economy would be stronger than ever. He urged his colleagues:

> We must use this tragedy as an opportunity to improve the quality of life for these residents of New Orleans and the Gulf Coast. For one-third of the people of the city of New Orleans to be living in poverty, sub-standard housing with poor healthcare, is inexcusable in this, the richest country in the world. We must raise living standards through job train-ing, better schools, and stronger neighborhoods and eradicate the hopeless conditions so many Americans live in not only in the Gulf region but throughout our Nation. Let us use this terrible storm to learn a lesson and commit us to a new war on poverty that will truly bring Americans who are living in 19th Century poverty into the 21st Century through better housing, healthcare, and education.[4]

Stafford Act Outlines Authority for Disaster Response

The Stafford Act is the main federal law enabling the federal government to respond to disasters. In special circumstances, such as hurricanes Katrina and Rita, Congress can pass additional laws authorizing further federal assistance.

In any major disaster, the President may—

(1) direct any Federal agency, with or without reimbursement, to utilize its authorities and the resources granted to it under Federal law (including personnel, equipment, supplies, facilities, and managerial, technical, and advisory services) in support of State and local assistance efforts;

(2) coordinate all disaster relief assistance (including voluntary assistance) provided by Federal agencies, private organizations, and State and local governments;

(3) provide technical and advisory assistance to affected State and local governments for—

(A) the performance of essential community services;

(B) issuance of warnings of risks and hazards;

(C) public health and safety information, including dissemination of such information;

(D) provision of health and safety measures; and

(E) management, control, and reduction of immediate threats to public health and safety; and

(4) assist State and local governments in the distribution of medicine, food, and other consumable supplies, and emergency assistance.

(a) In general

Federal agencies may on the direction of the President, provide assistance essential to meeting immediate threats to life and property resulting from a major disaster, as follows:

(1) Federal resources, generally

Utilizing, lending, or donating to State and local governments Federal equipment, supplies, facilities, personnel, and other resources, other than the extension of credit, for use or distribution by such governments in accordance with the purposes of this chapter.

(2) Medicine, food, and other consumables

Distributing or rendering through State and local governments, the American

National Red Cross, the Salvation Army, the Mennonite Disaster Service, and other relief and disaster assistance organizations medicine, food, and other consumable supplies, and other services and assistance to disaster victims.

(3) Work and services to save lives and protect property

Performing on public or private lands or waters any work or services essential to saving lives and protecting and preserving property or public health and safety, including—

    (A) debris removal;

    (B) search and rescue, emergency medical care, emergency mass care, emergency shelter, and provision of food, water, medicine, and other essential needs, including movement of supplies or persons;

    (C) clearance of roads and construction of temporary bridges necessary to the performance of emergency tasks and essential community services;

    (D) provision of temporary facilities for schools and other essential community services;

    (E) demolition of unsafe structures which endanger the public;

    (F) warning of further risks and hazards;

    (G) dissemination of public information and assistance regarding health and safety measures;

    (H) provision of technical advice to State and local governments on disaster management and control; and

    (I) reduction of immediate threats to life, property, and public health and safety.

(4) Contributions

Making contributions to State or local governments or owners or operators of private nonprofit facilities for the purpose of carrying out the provisions of this subsection.

(b) Federal share

The Federal share of assistance under this section shall be not less than 75 percent of the eligible cost of such assistance.

Source: 42 U.S. Congress, sections 5170a-5170b.

The federal government's handling of Katrina gave further ammunition to critics of the Bush administration. Although the House of Representatives had just approved the $50 billion aid package, Representative Dennis Kucinich accused the administration of indifference to the plight of Katrina victims:

> The President said a couple of hours ago that the Gulf Coast looks like it has been obliterated by a weapon. It has. Indifference is a weapon of mass destruction. Our indifferent government is in a crisis of legitimacy.[5]

Previously, the main rallying point of the administration's critics had been the ongoing war in Iraq. When Katrina hit, many of the National Guard troops who ordinarily could have gone to the Gulf Coast to assist in relief efforts were in fact stationed near the Persian Gulf and fighting in Iraq. Kucinich blamed the slow recovery effort on the nation's involvement in the Iraq war:

> As our government continues to squander the human and monetary resources of this country on the war, people are beginning to ask: Is it not time we begin to take care of our people here at home? Is it not time that we rescue our own citizens? Is it not time that we feed our own people? Is it not time that we shelter our own people? Is it not time that we provide physical and economic security for our own people? . . . The time is now to bring back to the United States the 78,000 National Guard troops currently deployed overseas. Many of our troops are already stationed in the wrong Gulf.[6]

Other Democrats joined in criticizing the government for prioritizing Iraq over Katrina relief. Representative Nick Rahall of West Virginia took particular issue with the use of U.S. funds to rebuild Iraq:

> Can't we afford America? We have spent more than $300 billion in Iraq and Afghanistan, yet this Republican Congress

Army National Guard soldiers help New Orleans residents into buses after they had been stranded for three nights at a hotel during Hurricane Katrina. Many blamed the slow recovery effort on U.S. involvement in Iraq, which meant that many of the National Guard troops who ordinarily could have assisted on the Gulf Coast were instead deployed outside of the country.

doesn't have a concrete plan to rebuild New Orleans, or the budget blueprint to do it. We are investing billions of American taxpayer dollars for bridges, levees, and infrastructure in Baghdad, yet we can't get a commitment from our leaders to rebuild the levees in New Orleans for Americans.[7]

Katrina's victims feel abandoned by the federal government.

In the days after the storm, frustrated New Orleanians wondered why the federal government was not providing aid more rapidly and efficiently. The city's director of homeland security, Colonel Terry Ebert, told the *New York Times*:

We are like little birds with our mouths open and you don't have to be very smart to know where to drop the worm. It's criminal within the confines of the United States that within one hour of the hurricane they weren't force-feeding us. It's like FEMA has never been to a hurricane.[8]

Although Congress had appropriated about $70 billion in hurricane-related aid to the Gulf Coast before adjourning for the holidays in December, that amount was far short of the $200 billion requested by Louisiana and Mississippi politicians. In a speech to the New Orleans City Council, Governor Blanco criticized the amount of the aid package:

Before Congress adjourned, they approved an aid package for the Gulf Coast area hit by Katrina. We all know it's not enough . . . but we will make the best we can with what we have received so far and keep fighting for our fair share of the recovery dollars. . . .

Right after I thank them for the help they've sent so far, I will remind them of the scope of Katrina's damage. I'll tell them that they've made a good start helping us recover and that Louisiana deserves more.

We are Americans. We will not be treated like second-class citizens.[9]

Many in the region have stressed that Katrina was a disaster that struck not only the Gulf Coast, but in fact the entire nation. In a report calling for increased federal assistance to the region, Democratic congressmen Gene Taylor of Mississippi and Charlie Melancon of Louisiana emphasized the need for "construction of a comprehensive hurricane protection and coastal restoration plan for the Gulf Coast."[10] They called for the construction to be funded by a "reliable, dedicated funding stream combined with flexible guidelines on the use of federal grants" because "the normal appropriations process is simply inadequate to meet funding needs for this endeavor."[11] In other words, general government programs, such as housing assistance administered by the U.S. Department of Housing and Urban Development (HUD), were not sufficient to help the Gulf Coast.

In justifying their call for special programs designed specifically for the Gulf Coast, Representatives Taylor and Melancon noted the importance that the region has played in the national economy, especially in oil and natural gas production. Noting that exploration for oil and gas has damaged wetlands in the area, thus making the region even more susceptible to hurricane damage, the congressmen asserted, "America's wetlands have paid the price for supplying this nation with the energy that moves commerce and people."[12]

Speaking before a subcommittee of Congress, Governor Blanco reminded committee members of the importance of New Orleans to the nation's economy:

> America's economy must have a vibrant commercial port at the mouth of the Mississippi River, its most important waterway. South Louisiana is the center point of the nation's energy economy. This is the export hub of the nation's breadbasket. This region fills the nation's restaurants and supermarkets with seafood. Indeed, the quality of life of our country depends on a vibrant Louisiana economy. Just as the nation recreated the economic greatness of New York City after 9-11, the nation needs New Orleans and South Louisiana.[13]

Damages caused by large-scale disasters impede the ability of localities and states to recover.

Before Hurricane Katrina, the federal model for disaster response relied upon local and state governments as the first-line responders, with people at the "ground level" responsible for requesting federal assistance needed, and the federal government responding accordingly. Although the federal government lent assistance, local governments and states bore most of the responsibility, both for preparedness and recovery. The widespread devastation caused by Hurricane Katrina was unprecedented: A major city was virtually wiped off the map overnight, and the surrounding region was left with little upon which to rebuild. As congressmen Taylor and Melancon explained:

> The Gulf Coast must also cope with the reality of high costs associated with completing large-scale hurricane protection and coastal restoration projects. The tremendous amount of design, engineering, and construction work these monumental projects require is certainly within the ability of the professionals that have been working on this issue. However, the decimated state of Gulf Coast economies handicaps their ability to meet the fiscal obligations necessary to complete these projects in a timely manner.[14]

The Senate report recommended maintaining local and state governments as the first line of responsibility but also recognized the need to increase federal responsibility in preparing for and responding to natural disasters. For example, the report suggested that the Department of Homeland Security, the Army Corps of Engineers, and other federal agencies should:

> ... establish an interagency review board, including state and local officials, to examine the level of vulnerability of communities located in floodplains and coastal regions, to hurricanes and floods, and specifically examine the adequacy of existing and planned flood and hurricane protection levees and flood control structures, the contribution of environmental and ecological conditions, and the impact of nonstructural programs, such as the federal flood insurance program and pre- and post-disaster mitigation programs.[15]

In other words, the Senate Committee suggested that the federal government should carefully evaluate the large areas of the country that are susceptible to natural disasters and, working with local and state governments, take steps to reduce the risk.

Senate Report on Katrina

The Senate report on Katrina assigned blame to all levels of government, but faulted the federal government in particular for not scaling its initial response to the immense magnitude of Katrina:

Effective response to mass emergencies is a critical role of every level of government. It is a role that requires an unusual level of planning, coordination and dispatch among governments' diverse units. Following the terrorist attacks of 9/11, this country went through one of the most sweeping reorganizations of federal government in history. While driven primarily by concerns of terrorism, the reorganization was designed to strengthen our nation's ability to address the consequences of both natural and man-made disasters. In its first major test, this reorganized system failed. Katrina revealed that much remains to be done. . . .

It has long been standard practice that emergency response begins at the lowest possible jurisdictional level—typically the local government, with state government becoming involved at the local government's request when the resources of local government are (or are expected to be) overwhelmed. Similarly, while the federal government provides ongoing financial support to state and local governments for emergency preparedness, ordinarily it becomes involved in responding to a disaster at a state's request when resources of state and local governments are (or are expected to be) overwhelmed. Louisiana's Emergency Operations Plan explicitly lays out this hierarchy of response.

During a catastrophe, which by definition almost immediately exceeds state and local resources and significantly disrupts governmental operations and emergency services, the role of the federal government is particularly vital, and it would reasonably be expected to play a more substantial role in response than in an "ordinary" disaster.

Source: U.S. Senate Committee on Homeland Security and Governmental Affairs, *Hurricane Katrina: A Nation Still Unprepared* (May 2006), 2–3.

Hurricane Katrina so disabled the Gulf Coast region that local communities could not carry out day-to-day duties, let alone recover from the damage. In a speech to business leaders, Governor Blanco called on the federal government to financially support the operations of these communities as they recovered, saying:

> Just Tuesday, Mayor Nagin announced that his city teeters on the edge of bankruptcy . . . that he will lay off 3,000 city workers. This is why I've asked President Bush and Congressional leaders to change the rules of the Stafford Disaster Relief and Emergency Assistance Act. We need to allow federal aid money to cover more than just overtime for public employees. Our cities and parishes need to make payroll. They must pay the men and women who provide those basic services and changing the Stafford Act will allow them to provide those basic services.[16]

Summary

Americans responded to hurricanes Katrina and Rita with unprecedented generosity, sending money, needed supplies, and volunteers. Nonprofit organizations, such as the Red Cross and Salvation Army, came to the rescue, but the combined efforts of nonprofits and individuals cannot meet the demands of a future disaster anywhere near the scale of Hurricane Katrina. The federal government alone has the financial and other resources necessary to respond to large-scale disasters, and many people believe that the federal government must improve its capacity to respond to future disasters.

Local and State Governments Should Accept More Responsibility for Disaster Preparedness and Relief

In the days immediately after Hurricane Katrina, New Orleans mayor Ray Nagin was widely featured in the national media, particularly for his sharp criticism of the federal government's reaction to the disaster. During an interview, local radio correspondent Garland Robinette asked Mayor Nagin what he needed to regain control of the situation in New Orleans. An angry Nagin replied:

> I need 500 buses, man. We ain't talking about—you know, one of the briefings we had, they were talking about getting public school bus drivers to come down here and bus people out [of] here.
>
> I'm like, "You got to be kidding me. This is a national disaster. Get every doggone Greyhound bus line in the country and get [them] moving to New Orleans.[17]

Throughout the interview, Nagin criticized the federal government for failing to provide the assistance the city needed.

In an era in which the media is increasingly dominated by short sound bites and blogging, and in which technology makes satellite photographs widely available through the Internet, Mayor Nagin's words quickly came back to haunt him. Bloggers posted satellite images of more than 400 buses—146 transit buses, plus 255 school buses—that lay partially submerged in parking lots nearby and had not been used to evacuate city residents. Critics quickly dubbed the parking lot full of buses the "Mayor Ray Nagin Memorial Motor Pool."

Nagin and high-profile figures such as Reverend Jesse Jackson sharply criticized the federal government for its failures to respond effectively to Katrina. Some questioned whether the federal government was insensitive to the plight of people in New Orleans because many of the people who did not evacuate prior to the storm were poor African Americans. Other leaders, however, questioned whether local and state politicians should rely on the federal government to prepare for and respond to large-scale disasters. In a strongly-worded statement, conservative African-American minister Jesse Lee Peterson called for stronger leadership and self-reliance: "Black people died not because of President Bush or racism, they died because of their unhealthy dependence on the government and the incompetence of Mayor Ray Nagin and Governor Kathleen Blanco."[18]

Although not necessarily speaking as harshly as Peterson, many people share the belief that people should not rely on the federal government to protect them from disasters, but should instead demand accountability from local and state leaders, who have better knowledge of the unique problems that an area faces. New Orleans is frequently described as a "bowl shaped" city; it is located below sea level. Despite federal support for developing evacuation plans, however, neither the city nor the state had an effective plan to get people out of New Orleans as Katrina approached. Proponents of greater local and state responsibility

New Orleans mayor Ray Nagin gestures at a news confer-
ence in January 2007. Nagin was highly critical of the
federal government's response to the havoc wreaked by
Hurricane Katrina in August 2005.

argue that the federal government cannot prepare and coordinate local responses. Many of the people affected by Hurricane
Katrina have recognized the need for significant changes at the
local and state level.

The federal government is too large and unwieldy to have responsibility.

Federal government investigations into the response to Katrina
concluded that FEMA had mishandled its responsibilities. It
was thus recommended that major changes take place within
the organization. Although they agreed that FEMA's response

to Katrina was inefficient, West Virginia University professors Russell Sobel and Peter Leeson, authors of *Flirting with Disaster*, argued, "the best reform Congress could undertake would be to decentralize and depoliticize the task of disaster relief management by taking the federal government out of the disaster relief process altogether."[19]

THE LETTER OF THE LAW

Governors Must Ask President to Declare a Disaster Area

The balance of responsibilities between the states and the federal government is reflected in the Stafford Act, the main federal law dealing with disaster relief. In this provision, the law clearly puts responsibility on the states to respond to disasters. A state may call in the federal government's assistance only if the state is overwhelmed.

All requests for a declaration by the President that a major disaster exists shall be made by the Governor of the affected State. Such a request shall be based on a finding that the disaster is of such severity and magnitude that effective response is beyond the capabilities of the State and the affected local governments and that Federal assistance is necessary. As part of such request, and as a prerequisite to major disaster assistance under this chapter, the Governor shall take appropriate response action under State law and direct execution of the State's emergency plan. The Governor shall furnish information on the nature and amount of State and local resources which have been or will be committed to alleviating the results of the disaster, and shall certify that, for the current disaster, State and local government obligations and expenditures (of which State commitments must be a significant proportion) will comply with all applicable cost-sharing requirements of this chapter. Based on the request of a Governor under this section, the President may declare under this chapter that a major disaster or emergency exists.

Source: 42 U.S.C., section 5170.

With its vast financial resources and hundreds of thousands of employees, the federal government might seem to be the logical choice to respond to disasters. But many people believe that, as an extension of the people of 50 states and the District of Columbia, the federal government should not have primary responsibility for responding to disasters that strike one area of the country. People who make this argument generally are not concerned solely with disaster relief, but believe that across the board, the federal government should be smaller and spend less money. Opponents of "big government" are typically aligned with the Republican Party or the Libertarian Party, the latter of which attracts a small number of voters and has elected candidates in some states.

These opponents of big government are often motivated by the desire to pay less money in federal taxes and the belief that excessive federal regulation interferes with business and with personal freedom. For example, the Cato Institute, a libertarian think tank, argues that "increasing federal control over infrastructure projects, such as the New Orleans levees, that could be better managed by state, local, and private interests" is "worrisome."[20]

Such arguments against an increasingly large federal government have a solid historical foundation. When the founders of the U.S. government wrote the Constitution in 1791, they established a framework in which the federal government had a few "enumerated" (carefully spelled out) powers, such as the power to form an army to defend the nation from foreign enemies, the power to print money, and the power to regulate interstate commerce (business transactions across state lines). The powers that were not given to the federal government were generally "reserved" for the states, although the Bill of Rights granted to individuals certain rights, which limited what states could do. Generally speaking, however, the federal government had little power, while the states had "police power." With applications much broader than criminal matters alone, police power means the ability to pass any laws that the state deems necessary for the good of its people, subject to limits imposed by the Constitution or by federal laws that fit within the federal government's power.

Outside of the military, the federal government did not have much of an infrastructure—facilities, equipment, financial reserves, or employees—for much of the first 150 years of the nation's existence. A constitutional amendment in 1913 was necessary for the federal government to collect taxes based on individuals' income (as opposed to collecting taxes that were "apportioned" according to each state's population). The "New Deal" of the 1930s, a series of reforms championed by President Franklin Delano Roosevelt, changed the balance of power between the states and the federal government dramatically. Reacting to the widespread poverty of the Great Depression, the Roosevelt administration created a number of projects around the country, with the underlying purpose of creating jobs for unemployed Americans. Under the authority of new federal agencies, such as the Tennessee Valley Authority and the Works Progress Administration, the federal government built roads, public buildings, dams, power plants, and other facilities.

Although these projects benefited many people, expending federal resources for local projects was a change of direction for the federal government. Today, spending by the federal government amounts to more than $2.5 trillion per year, which, according to the advocacy group Americans for Tax Reform, is equivalent to roughly 1 out of every 4 dollars earned by American workers.[21] The federal government employs nearly 2 million people (not including the U.S. Postal Service), and nearly 5 out of 6 federal employees works outside of the metropolitan area of Washington, D.C., according to the Bureau of Labor Statistics.[22]

Such a large government is, predictably, plagued by inefficiency in its response to disasters. Noting that FEMA reports to the Department of Homeland Security, the president, and Congress, Sobel and Leeson write, "With so many political decision makers involved in the actions of FEMA, it is easy for relief efforts to be slowed or stalled and resources allocated to less important uses."[23] Sobel and Leeson contrasted the inefficiency of the federal government's activities to the performance of Wal-Mart, which sought to provide needed supplies in the regions hit by Katrina: "While FEMA was scrambling to respond, Wal-Mart was providing the items rescue workers and victims needed, in the right quantities, at their everyday low prices, and sometimes even for free."[24] The difference, they write, was that "Wal-Mart ... had an incentive to act fast since failing to do so would result in forgone profits to the company."[25]

State and local governments must improve disaster planning and response.

The consensus opinion appears to be that the response to Hurricane Katrina represented a failure at all levels of government—local, state, and federal. Although proponents of a limited federal government would argue that federal failures were inevitable, many believe that local and state governments also made mistakes that could have been avoided through better preparation. Unlike the Cato Institute, which has called for a complete abandonment of the federal role in disaster relief, the Heritage Foundation, a think tank aligned with conservative Republicans, argues that the federal government should take a more supportive role, with the local and state governments taking the lead in planning for and responding to disasters "because state and local officials know the needs of their communities best and are well-placed to provide immediate, on-the-ground response following disasters."[26] The group envisions the federal government's role as providing resources specifically requested by localities or states.

Speaking at an event sponsored by the Heritage Foundation, Texas Governor Rick Perry expressed support for the idea that local and state governments could benefit by improving their own disaster readiness:

Federalizing disaster response begs a couple of questions: If the federal response to Hurricane Katrina was, as President Bush agreed, inadequate, then how am I supposed to explain to the people of Port Arthur, Galveston, Brownsville, Corpus Christi, and Houston that it is a good thing that Washington will take over the next time? And if the federal response to Katrina—a natural disaster that we knew was coming for several days—was too slow, how on earth can the federal government provide an effective and immediate response if there is no warning before a radiological bomb goes off in

THE LETTER OF THE LAW

States Must Plan for Disasters

The federal government provides disaster assistance to local communities and states, but maintains a policy that local communities and states have the primary responsibility for disaster preparedness and relief. Under federal regulations based on the Stafford Act, to qualify for increased federal resources, a state must develop comprehensive "mitigation" plans to reduce damages in the case of disaster, although most forms of emergency assistance remain available regardless of whether states develop such plans.

Section 201.1
(a) The purpose of this part is to provide information on the policies and procedures for mitigation planning as required by the provisions of section 322 of the Stafford Act, 42 U.S.C. 5165.
(b) The purpose of mitigation planning is for State, local, and Indian tribal governments to identify the natural hazards that impact them, to identify actions and activities to reduce any losses from those hazards, and to establish a coordinated process to implement the plan, taking advantage of a wide range of resources.
Section 201.3
[Increased federal disaster planning assistance is available, based on a] demonstration that the State is committed to a comprehensive state mitigation program, which might include any of the following:

Dallas or a biological agent is let loose across the border from El Paso in Juarez?[27]

For years, the federal government has provided resources to help local and state governments prepare for disasters; some local and state governments have done better jobs than others. A report by the U.S. Senate Committee on Homeland Security and Governmental Affairs found that the state of Mississippi could have been better prepared for Katrina; but the report reserved its harshest criticism for local and state government officials

(i) A commitment to support local mitigation planning by providing workshops and training, State planning grants, or coordinated capability development of local officials, including Emergency Management and Floodplain Management certifications.

(ii) A statewide program of hazard mitigation through the development of legislative initiatives, mitigation councils, formation of public/private partnerships, and/or other executive actions that promote hazard mitigation.

(iii) The State provides a portion of the non-Federal match for [the federal Hazard Mitigation Grant Program] and/or other mitigation projects.

(iv) To the extent allowed by State law, the State requires or encourages local governments to use a current version of a nationally applicable model building code or standard that addresses natural hazards as a basis for design and construction of State sponsored mitigation projects.

(v) A comprehensive, multi-year plan to mitigate the risks posed to existing buildings that have been identified as necessary for post-disaster response and recovery operations.

(vi) A comprehensive description of how the State integrates mitigation into its post-disaster recovery operations.

Source: 44 C.F.R., section 201.

in Louisiana. The report concluded, "the City of New Orleans, with primary responsibility for evacuation of its citizens, had language in its plan stating the city's intent to assist those who needed transportation for pre-storm evacuation, but had no actual plan provisions to implement that intent."[28]

The report found that the state of Louisiana, which could have assisted the city, was no better prepared, noting:

> The Louisiana Department of Transportation and Development, whose secretary had personally accepted departmental responsibility under the state's emergency operations plan to arrange for transportation for evacuation in emergencies, had done nothing to prepare for that responsibility prior to Katrina.[29]

Overall, according to the report:

> The Louisiana Office of Homeland Security and Emergency Preparedness suffered problems such as inadequate funding; not enough staff; insufficient training; widespread lack of understanding of . . . unified command; an overall lack of preparation; and a lack of emergency-management capacity to respond effectively to Katrina.[30]

Many in areas affected by Katrina recognize the need for local and state improvement.

Long before the Senate report found flaws in Mississippi's disaster response, the government of Mississippi had already begun intensive efforts to improve its future ability to respond to disasters. In Mississippi, a state in which the Republican Party holds considerable power, many politicians, though grateful for federal assistance, have taken the position that the people of Mississippi should rely on themselves and their local and state governments to a larger degree than they rely on the federal government. Republican Governor Haley Barbour appointed an independent Governor's Commission on Recovery, Rebuilding, and Renewal to study how to recover from the devastation caused by Katrina and how to improve the state's response to future natural disasters. The commission produced a detailed report with nearly 200 pages of recommendations. Introducing the report, the commission noted of the recommendations it was making:

> Some are appeals for aid beyond Mississippi's borders, but most are proposals to cities, towns, and counties, who have the most to say about how citizens live, work, and play in their communities. They write the zoning and building codes. They choose whether or not to join regional transportation, infrastructure, or economic development initiatives.[31]

While high-profile Louisiana politicians such as Governor Blanco and Mayor Nagin have been sharply critical of the federal government's response to Katrina, Governor Barbour has been publicly supportive of the federal response to Katrina. During his annual State of the State address to the state legislature in January 2006, Barbour said:

> There has been plenty of controversy about the federal role in relief and recovery. While it hasn't been perfect, and in fact couldn't be, the federal agencies have done a lot more right than wrong. The Coast Guard's helicopter crews, the U.S. Department of Transportation's fuel supplies, the Seabees and their expertise all made a huge difference at critical times.
> The President has repeatedly extended deadlines for emergency relief and debris removal that provide hundreds of millions of federal assistance dollars. The Bush Administration proposed an unprecedented package of assistance to help the states and people affected by Katrina. And on behalf of a grateful state, I thank President Bush. . . . The United States government has never given anything like this much money

or nearly this much latitude to a state as Mississippi receives under this legislation.[32]

He also expressed gratitude to those outside of Mississippi who willingly helped the state in its recovery efforts:

> Corporate America and small businesses, philanthropists and everyday citizens have been incredibly generous . . . but I must single out the churches and faith-based groups, who were there on day one and are still there in meaningful numbers today. Theirs were the most powerful and productive efforts . . . And I'd be remiss not to mention the crucial contributions of our sister states. Those Governors, Democrats and Republicans, sent us their state's resources in an unprecedented manner, and they made a difference.[33]

He reserved his greatest praise for the people of Mississippi for the primary responsibility for the recovery efforts. Crediting "the spirit of Mississippians," he noted:

> Our people didn't whine or mope around; they're not into victimhood. Immediately after the storm passed through, they hitched up their britches and began helping themselves and helping their neighbors. The stories of ordinary people performing extraordinary acts of courage and selflessness are extremely common. The first responders, law enforcement, national guard, and military; but also neighbors helping neighbors, churches helping the needy, and poor people more interested in others getting assistance. That Mississippi spirit was obvious to people across the country and around the world.[34]

In Barbour's view, the actions of local government, both in the hours leading up to Katrina and in the months after the disaster, show that local and state governments can make

White House Report on Katrina

Overall, the White House report on the Katrina response was not as critical as the Senate report. The White House report explained the role of the federal government in disaster response in the context of federalism:

> The Founders created a constitutional framework in which each State, upon ratification of the Constitution, ceded some of its powers to the Federal government to create one united yet limited central government. The Constitution sets forth the specific and delegated powers that delineate Federal and State roles. It tells us which branches and offices will be part of the Federal government, what powers they may exercise, and what limitations constrain them. The Constitution also respects State powers by reserving those powers not given to the Federal government to the States or to the people. Our Federal system provides a structure to enable coordination between the United States government and State governments to create a balance that respects the sovereignty of both entities.
>
> The United States has long operated on the general premise that governments exist to do those things that individuals, alone or in free and voluntary association (e.g., families and charities), are not best positioned to do for themselves, such as ensuring public safety and providing law enforcement. Following these principles, the Founders created the Federal government to do those things that States cannot or should not do individually, such as defending the Nation, conducting foreign relations, and ensuring open and free interstate commerce. Accordingly, State and local governments assume the first and foremost line of defense against civil disturbance and threats to public safety. The Federal government guarantees its assistance to protect the States in their existence as representative republican governments from the external threat of invasion or attack, and against internal subversion or rebellion. Federal laws reinforce the concept that the Federal government should respect State sovereignty. For example, section 331 of the Insurrection Act requires the State legislature or, in its absence, the State governor, to make a formal request of the Federal government before the President may send in Federal troops to assist State efforts to restore order.

Source: The White House, *The Federal Response to Katrina: Lessons Learned* (February 2006), 11 (footnotes omitted).

an enormous difference in disaster preparedness and recovery. He said:

> I salute the local elected officials who stayed put, made deci-
> sions before as well as after Katrina. Those decisions saved
> lives, as did the thousands of inland families who took in
> friends and family before the hurricane struck. The death toll,
> while large, was remarkably low compared to the enormity
> of the devastation; the decisiveness of local officials in order-
> ing evacuations played a major role in that. And those local
> officials deserve immense credit for the fact that continuity of
> government never broke down in Mississippi as it could have.
> Those local governments stood tall, and we are going to stand
> with them, now and in the future.[35]

One theme that ran through Mississippi's reaction to the devastation of Hurricane Katrina was a feeling that many of the losses could have been prevented if the state had learned its lessons from Hurricane Camille in 1969. That storm killed 130 people and destroyed 3,800 homes in Mississippi. Subsequently, a state-appointed commission made a number of recommen-dations, but they were largely ignored. As was observed by the commission that Governor Barbour formed after Katrina, the local governments were "concerned about imposing anything on constituents already beaten down by the hurricane."[36]

The post-Katrina commission's report made clear that Mis-sissippi must learn its lesson this time, stating:

> The rules we put off enacting and enforcing would have kept
> many out of harm's way and would have made buildings
> more resilient to high winds and high water. The hard choices
> we ducked in 1970 await us in 2006, only with more zeroes
> on the price tags.[37]

Acting in part on the commission's recommendations, the Mis-sissippi legislature passed a law requiring the coastal counties most ravaged by Katrina to adopt new building codes that reflect international recommendations for protecting structures against wind and flood damage. These new building requirements would impose additional costs on homeowners rebuilding their storm-damaged homes, and on those people building new homes in the coastal region; however, the new requirements would also prevent future storm damage from being as severe as it was during Katrina.

Summary

Although Katrina demonstrated the federal government's weaknesses in responding to disasters, not everyone is convinced that expanding the capacity of the federal government is the answer to preventing another Katrina. Opponents of "big government" oppose federal initiatives on the grounds that the federal government is too bureaucratic and inefficient to respond to local problems. Others believe that local governments and the states should devote more resources to disaster planning, while the federal role should be limited to responding in more flexible ways to specific requests made at the local or state level.

Federal Financial Assistance to Disaster Victims Is Inadequate

I n January 2007, Louisiana Governor Blanco, like many Americans, watched President George W. Bush deliver his annual State of the Union address. Like many in the Gulf Coast region, she was shocked that the president did not even mention the continued recovery from hurricanes Katrina and Rita. She was especially angry because, in the previous week, former FEMA head Michael Brown had made some disturbing allegations against the Bush administration. Many had accused the administration of playing favorites with Mississippi, which was headed by a Republican governor, over Louisiana and its Democratic administration. At a speech at New York Metropolitan College, which has a disaster management graduate program, the ousted Brown said, "Certain people in the White House were thinking we had to federalize Louisiana because [Kathleen Blanco is] a white, female Democratic governor and we have a chance to rub her nose in it."[38]

In a speech responding to President Bush's State of the Union address, Governor Blanco outlined what she perceived as unfair treatment of Louisiana residents:

> Louisiana had nearly 80% of the storm damage from two hurricanes received only 55% of federal relief funds. Mississippi, with 23% of the damage, received 45% of the relief funds.
>
> This is far more money proportionately, and they received it a full six months ahead of us. Our Road Home progress was delayed six months due to this disparity. . . .
>
> Earlier this month, FEMA announced the Katrina Cottage housing program. Mississippi has 31,000 families living in trailers, and received $280 million in funding for Katrina Cottages. Louisiana has 64,000 families living in trailers, but FEMA gave us only $74 million. . . .
>
> A few days ago, Secretary Leavitt called to tell me that Louisiana would only receive 45% of the funding for hospitals. This is unbelievable, considering Louisiana lost 97% of our hospital beds along the Gulf Coast. Mississippi got 38% of the funding, even though they only lost 3% of the Gulf Coast hospital beds. They lost only 79 beds to our more than 2,600 beds. . . .
>
> Louisiana and Mississippi both received $95 million for higher education. This is outrageous, considering Louisiana had 76%, or 84,000, of the displaced students, and three times as many universities as Mississippi. . . .
>
> Both Louisiana and Mississippi received $100 million for displaced K–12 students, in spite of the fact that Louisiana had 69%, or 176,000 of the displaced students. This is compared to Mississippi's 31%.[39]

In a letter to Speaker of the House Nancy Pelosi, asking her to launch a federal investigation into the distribution of disaster relief funds, Governor Blanco made it clear that the issue was not over-funding of Mississippi, but under-funding of Louisiana. She wrote:

Michael Brown, then director of the Federal Emergency Management Agency, was photographed in May 2005. Brown was accused of severely mismanaging the federal response to Hurricane Katrina; in turn, he later criticized the politics which, according to him, influenced FEMA's reaction.

We do not begrudge the battered citizens of Mississippi one nickel that has been allocated to meet their needs. We appreciated the generosity of the help that has been given. However, I am certain that most members of Congress would agree that the people of Louisiana are not second-class citizens and deserve proportionate relief. We are American citizens.[40]

Although the federal government approved more than $100 billion in disaster relief in response to Katrina and Rita, critics say that it was simply not enough. Various federal agencies received additional funding to aid in the recovery efforts, but most of the direct financial assistance to individuals, families, and communities is distributed through FEMA and the U.S. Small Business Administration (SBA):

- FEMA, through the Individuals and Households Program (IHP), provides monetary and other types of help to disaster victims. This money is intended for short-term needs, such as temporary housing, food, clothing, and medical expenses, and does not have to be repaid. FEMA also offers homeowners assistance in making minimal repairs needed to allow people to return to their homes—such as putting tarps over holes in roofs.

- The U.S. Small Business Administration (SBA) offers low-interest loans for long-term disaster relief, particularly rebuilding homes.

Critics of these federal programs say that the government should distribute financial assistance more efficiently, that more help from the government is needed to help homeowners who did not have insurance to rebuild their homes, and that the government must help communities rebuild on many levels.

Disaster assistance is needed to protect those who do not have insurance.

Writing for the Urban Institute, Susan Popkin and two colleagues noted that New Orleans had a relatively high percentage of homeowners who had paid off their mortgages and owned their homes outright. When homeowners owe money on a mortgage, they are required by the lender to maintain homeowner's insurance, because the lender has a legal interest in the property; the lender can foreclose on (seize) the property if the homeowner does not pay the mortgage. Because of this, the lender wants to protect its financial interests in case the home is destroyed or damaged. Popkin and her colleagues concluded, "Without mortgages, many low-income longtime homeowners opted out of costly homeowner's insurance or flood insurance."[41] Additionally, they noted that many people in the areas affected by Katrina and Rita were not required to purchase flood insurance because they were not in designated high-risk flood zones—this included many residents of areas protected by the federally-constructed levees that failed.

These problems were particularly severe in New Orleans's Lower Ninth Ward neighborhood. That area was inhabited almost entirely by African Americans, many of whom were living below the poverty level. Unlike most poor African-American communities, however, the Lower Ninth Ward had a high level of home-ownership. According to the Urban Institute report, 62 percent of the neighborhood's residents were homeowners, and nearly half owned their homes outright, as Popkin and her colleagues observed: "Many of these families had lived in their shotgun-style houses for generations and owned them outright—only 52 percent had a current mortgage and the homeowner's insurance that lenders require." Additionally, they observed, the neighborhood was not in an area in which flood insurance was required for those with federally backed mortgages, resulting in low participation in the program, and as a result, "[t]hese uninsured low-income households lack the wherewithal to rebuild their homes."[42]

At the time of the 2005 hurricanes, the federal government's primary method of assisting uninsured homeowners was to provide low-interest loans through the Small Business Administration. A report by the NAACP's Gulf Coast Advocacy Center called on the federal government to change this policy: "Much of the assistance provided, like that from the Small Business Administration, is unattainable for low-income households, who often have difficulty meeting repayment conditions. Additional funds must be provided to address this need."[43]

Rudolph Penner of the Urban Institute argues that expecting insurance coverage to replace disaster assistance is unrealistic. Noting the longstanding precedent of politicians providing disaster assistance, "along with a natural human tendency to underestimate risk," he argues, "selling voluntary, unsubsidized insurance [is] difficult."[44] In other words, people do not think that they are going to be affected by a disaster, and if so, they expect the government to take care of them. Therefore, they are unlikely to buy insurance, especially if the government does not step in to make it more affordable.

Rapid assistance is necessary in the aftermath of a major disaster.

In the immediate aftermath of a disaster, people have many needs, such as obtaining food, replacement clothing, medications, and other necessities. Rather than evaluating people's needs on a case-by-case basis, FEMA provides a set amount—for Katrina, it was $2,000—to individuals who apply for aid. An applicant signs up for this aid by giving his or her Social Security number and an address in a federally declared disaster area. In doing this, FEMA can quickly distribute money to address individuals' short-term needs, then evaluate requests for further assistance on a case-by-case basis. Typically, FEMA distributes this aid either through mailing a check or directly depositing the money into a person's bank account. By law, the money is to be spent on disaster-related necessities.

Congress Appropriates More than $50 Billion in Hurricane Relief

Having already approved more than $10 billion in hurricane relief, Congress passed a package including more than $50 billion in spending on the Gulf Coast recovery effort.

What follows is the Congressional Research Service summary of the law, not the actual text of the law.

Second Emergency Supplemental Appropriations Act to Meet Immediate Needs Arising From the Consequences of Hurricane Katrina, 2005—

Appropriates an additional $1.4 billion to the Department of Defense-Military for "Operation and Maintenance, Defense-Wide" for emergency hurricane expenses, to support costs of evacuation, emergency repairs, deployment of personnel, and other costs resulting from immediate relief efforts, to remain available through FY [fiscal year] 2006. Allows the transfer of up to $6 million to the Armed Forces Retirement Home for emergency hurricane expenses.

Authorizes the Secretary of Defense to transfer these funds to appropriations for military personnel, operation and maintenance, procurement, family housing, Defense Health Program, and working capital funds. Requires transferred funds to be merged with and be available for the same purposes and for the same time period as the appropriation or fund to which transferred. Requires re-transfer back to this appropriation of any transferred funds determined to be not necessary for the purposes of this Act.

Directs the Secretary to notify the congressional defense committees in writing within five days after any such transfer.

Designates such amounts as emergency requirements which shall not count for budget enforcement purposes of the Congressional Budget Act of 1974.

Appropriates to the Department of the Army, Corps of Engineers—Civil, an additional $200 million for "Operation and Maintenance," and an additional $200 million for "Flood Control and Coastal Emergencies," to remain available until expended, for emergency expenses for repair of storm damage to authorized projects, as well as flood control and hurricane shore protection projects, in the Gulf States affected by Hurricane Katrina. Requires weekly reports by the Chief of Engineers, acting through the Assistant Secretary of the Army for Civil Works, to the Committees on Appropriations on funds allocation and obligation.

Designates such amounts as emergency requirements which shall not count for budget enforcement purposes of the Congressional Budget Act of 1974.

Appropriates an additional $50 billion to the Department of Homeland Security for disaster relief (for areas affected by Hurricane Katrina), to remain available until expended, of which up to $100 million may be transferred to and merged with "Emergency Preparedness and Response—Public Health Programs" for the National Disaster Medical System to support medical care as authorized by the Public Health Security and Bioterrorism Preparedness and Response Act of 2002. Requires the transfer of $15 million to, and merger with, "Departmental Management and Operations—Office of Inspector General" for necessary expenses of the Office of Inspector General for audits and investigations as authorized by law for Hurricane Katrina response and recovery activities. Requires weekly reports by the Secretary of Homeland Security to the Committees on Appropriations on funds allocation and obligation.

Designates such amounts as emergency requirements which shall not count for budget enforcement purposes of the Congressional Budget Act of 1974.

(Sec. 101) Authorizes the use of the emergency procurement authority of the Office of Federal Procurement Policy Act by executive agencies to make purchases without obtaining competitive quotations for procurements of property or services determined by the agency head to be used in support of Hurricane Katrina rescue and relief operations, if an agency employee determines that the purchase price is reasonable.

Increases from $2,500 to $250,000 the maximum amount (micro-purchase threshold) of such a purchase that: (1) may be made without obtaining competitive quotations; and (2) need not be distributed equitably among qualified suppliers.

Source: Congressional Research Service, summary of Public Law No. 109-62 (2005).

Because of the widespread evacuations to locations throughout the nation, including many evacuees headed to Texas, FEMA used a new tactic to quickly get aid to people through its Expedited Assistance program. Because many people took refuge in large shelters in Texas and did not have easy access to mail or their bank accounts, the agency distributed emergency aid to about 10,000 people at Texas shelters in the form of $2,000 debit cards. The cards could be used anywhere that accepted Master-Card. At the time, Natalie Rule, FEMA's director of public affairs, said the program was experiencing initial success:

> Expedited cash assistance is getting critical aid to thousands of Hurricane Katrina victims across the nation. With the large share of expedited aid reaching victims nationwide through direct deposit and check, the additional delivery of aid through this piloted program has achieved exactly what we'd hoped to do—get needed dollars to those in some of the largest need shelters.[45]

Still, many were critical of how long it took this aid to reach the hands of people who were desperate just to survive. Republican Senator David Vitter of Louisiana criticized what he perceived as bureaucracy getting in the way of relief:

> Beyond the devastated area, the radius of our challenges has expanded to wherever there are large numbers of evacuees— Houston, San Antonio, Charlotte, Salt Like City, Milwaukee—and every town and city across the rest of Louisiana. You see, so many of the evacuees lived their lives paycheck to paycheck. So many others depended on Social Security or other programs. They need immediate help in all of those areas—well beyond Louisiana. Unfortunately, the bureaucrats are still in charge of this. . . .
>
> The tens of billions of dollars in government relief money through FEMA and the State [Office of Emergency

Preparedness]—the very same agencies which failed us—will lead to more failure.[46]

As the one-year anniversary of Katrina's landfall approached, many organizations released reports documenting the recovery efforts, particularly noting the federal government's role. Many expressed dissatisfaction with federal recovery efforts, despite the billions that had been allocated by Congress. In a report issued by the Mississippi chapter of the NAACP, Amy Liu of the Washington, D.C.–based Brookings Institution think tank wrote:

> While [at least $107 billion has] been invested in the Gulf region one year after Katrina, it is clear there remain significant gaps in the federal response to recovery. To date, low-income and working families, particularly in Mississippi, are being locked out from the bulk of the benefits of the recovery effort.[47]

Multiple streams of assistance are necessary for disaster recovery.

Although cash payments to disaster victims for their short-term needs are helpful, they are only one piece of the puzzle. Helping people get back onto their feet after a disaster on the scale of the 2005 hurricanes involves helping people and communities address many needs, including housing, education, and employment. Those involved in Gulf Coast recovery efforts have called for the federal government to assist people and communities with a broad approach involving multiple federal agencies and numerous forms of assistance.

Many advocates for housing opportunities for low-income people would prefer to have the U.S. Department of Housing and Urban Development (HUD) play an expanded role in meeting the needs of disaster evacuees. FEMA's inefficiencies in responding to housing needs have been well documented.

For example, the agency paid $900 million to purchase manufactured housing that it could not use because it did not meet the agency's own standards. FEMA then paid the city of Hope, Arkansas, rent in the amount of $300,000 per year for land to store unusable homes—land that had previously been rented to a hay farmer for $5,000 per year, according to the Senate report on the response to Katrina.

Groups including the National Low Income Housing Coalition (NLIHC) and ACORN, a national association of anti-poverty groups, have proposed that the housing needs of those displaced by Katrina and Rita be served by HUD's Disaster Voucher Program (DVP). Throughout the nation, HUD gives out two main forms of rental assistance for low-income people: Public Housing (or "housing projects"), government-owned housing for which low-income individuals and families are eligible; and Housing Choice Vouchers (or "Section 8"), which allow people to rent houses or apartments from private landlords, with HUD paying a major portion of the rent each month. People in either of these programs who lose their housing to a disaster become eligible for DVP, which operates much like the Section 8 program. The difference is that DVP allows people to rent housing throughout the nation, wherever they can find a landlord willing to rent to them.

By contrast, people who lived in homes that they owned or rented without HUD's assistance when Katrina and Rita struck were served by FEMA, not the DVP program. FEMA serves these people through a variety of approaches, including paying people's rent in apartments or hotels and providing people with temporary trailer homes. With an initial 18-month deadline for housing assistance, the housing advocacy groups wrote to FEMA, the Department of Homeland Security (which oversees FEMA), and HUD in October 2006, requesting that FEMA transfer responsibility for housing all evacuees to HUD, to be administered through DVP. The groups wrote:

Shifting responsibility for temporary rental assistance to HUD would take advantage of the agency's experience in administering housing assistance to people in need, as well as the infrastructure of local public housing agencies that already administer 2,000,000 vouchers nationwide. It would also provide more flexibility and choice for displaced families, security to landlords who rent to evacuees, and improved federal oversight of the use of federal resources.[48]

The federal government did not adopt the approach proposed by the groups, and continued to serve most evacuees' housing needs through FEMA. As the deadline for housing assistance loomed, the federal government announced in January 2007 that it would extend the deadline for housing assistance an additional six months. Many believed, however, that the six-month extension was inadequate. Groups such as ACORN and NLIHC pushed for at least three times that.

Low-income housing advocates have been disappointed with the federal government's long-term approach to housing, specifically rebuilding New Orleans and other areas affected by the 2005 hurricanes. In the Mississippi NAACP's report, Amy Liu noted that "Katrina has provided an opportunity to replace predominantly low-income neighborhoods with healthier, mixed-income communities, and the commitment to promoting mixed-income neighborhoods has been nearly nonexistent."[49] A report by the NAACP's Gulf Coast Advocacy Center contained several proposals for improving long-term housing opportunities for low-income people affected by the hurricane, including:

- Funding 13,500 affordable housing units by issuing federally-backed housing vouchers for 25 percent of the housing units developed through the government's Gulf Opportunity Zone program supporting the construction of rental housing; and

- Establishing "down-payment-assistance programs, and rent-to-own programs" to "assist families that had uninsured homes destroyed by the hurricane to return to ownership.[50]

Although much of disaster relief is focused on helping homeowners and families find temporary or new homes, children affected by disasters have complex needs. In a report by the Urban Institute, Olivia Golden noted that children evacuated from the area affected by Katrina had distinct psychological, medical, educational, nutritional, and financial needs, for which increased federal attention was necessary. Children in the disaster area refused to eat, were inattentive, feared strangers, and had been traumatized by being in floodwaters and seeing dead bodies. In New Orleans, Golden suggested, problems were complicated by the fact that so many children lived in poverty and that social services were inadequate even before the storm. The problem, she noted, was particularly severe for infants and toddlers:

> Before the hurricane, Louisiana's capacity to meet the needs of these young children was limited. Part of the problem is a national one: the United States has generally invested little in children below school age, and no service system takes responsibility for tracking how children are doing. . . .[51]

With New Orleans's young children already at a disadvantage, made far worse by the disaster, Golden proposed increasing the federal government's support of the Head Start program, including the Early Head Start program. Through Head Start, the federal government makes grants to public and private nonprofit and for-profit organizations to provide services to young children, including early math and reading education and meeting children's nutritional needs. The program targets children from low-income families. Golden noted that, because Head

In the aftermath of Hurricane Katrina, Louisiana governor Kathleen Blanco made rebuilding businesses and residences her priorities. In the photograph above, Governor Blanco speaks to the press on August 30, 2005.

Start is a national program, it was able to respond initially to the displacement of children by shifting funding to programs that served Katrina evacuees.

Golden called for the federal government to increase funding for Head Start programs in New Orleans from about $21 million to $56 million, allowing the program to expand the services that it offers, serve children from families just above the poverty level who are in need but do not meet income criteria for the program, and coordinate with other recovery efforts. She wrote:

> This strategy would give the city its best chance of helping young children recover from trauma and from lifelong poverty and disadvantage. Well coordinated with other dimensions of rebuilding, such as employment and neighborhood development, these new programs could be a powerful incentive for parents to move back to the city.[52]

In the immediate aftermath of Hurricane Katrina, Governor Blanco of Louisiana also made rebuilding businesses a priority. In an October 2005 speech, she told business leaders that she had asked Congress for $200 million in short-term loans for Louisiana businesses to keep them running. She also proposed a comprehensive package, which she said included:

- Up to 30 billion dollars in tax-exempt "Hurricane Recovery" bonds. This will dramatically lower the cost of capital to companies of all sizes.

- A job-creation tax credit will motivate large companies with significant payrolls to remain in the region.

- A 10 billion dollar Louisiana Business Development Fund to provide grants to small businesses that return to the affected areas of our state.[53]

Summary

Just as critics say that hurricanes Katrina and Rita exposed weaknesses in the federal government's ability to respond to natural disasters, many believe that the 2005 hurricanes also exposed weaknesses in the government's ability to help individuals, families, and communities recover. One of the major criticisms is that people are generally unprepared for a disaster of such magnitude and therefore unlikely to have the necessary insurance. Further, people with low incomes are less likely to be insured and will usually have a more difficult time rebuilding. Proponents of increased federal disaster assistance say that quickly getting money into the hands of disaster victims is particularly important, but that the federal government must also infuse money into rebuilding private housing, community assets, and businesses.

Federal Financial Assistance to Disaster Victims Is Wasteful

On January 24, 2007, a federal judge sentenced Lawanda Williams, an Alabama resident, to six years in a federal prison. Williams had defrauded the federal government of more than $267,000 by filing 28 claims for disaster relief following Hurricane Katrina. Although her own home in Alabama was not damaged by the storm, Williams filed claims using addresses for properties in Alabama, Florida, Louisiana, and Mississippi, which she did not own. She also used other people's Social Security numbers, and submitted false documentation to FEMA to support her claims.

In addition to the prison sentence, the judge ordered Williams to repay the federal government the full amount that she had stolen, and also ordered her to forfeit everything that she had purchased with the money, including four cars, a television, other electronic equipment, and real estate.

The Williams case was not an isolated incident. Deborah Rhodes, the U.S. attorney for the Southern District of Alabama, classified the prosecution of Williams as part of a concerted effort to punish those who took advantage of the government's disaster relief efforts. She said:

> Ms. Williams used Hurricane Katrina and the relief efforts as an opportunity to make hundreds of thousands of dollars by lying and by stealing other people's identities. The Hurricane Katrina Fraud Task Force is actively working to bring to justice those who took advantage of the recovery efforts to enrich themselves.[54]

Although the task forced assembled by U.S. Attorney General Alberto Gonzalez stepped up efforts to prosecute fraud related to Katrina, many perpetrators remain at large. A report by the U.S. Government Accountability Office (GAO) estimated that the federal government paid between $600 million and $1.4 billion in disaster relief funds to people making fraudulent claims. This amount represents about 16 percent of the money that the government spent on disaster relief. A later report by the GAO revealed:

> As of November 2006, FEMA had detected through its own processes about $290 million in overpayments and had collected nearly $7 million of the about $290 million identified as improper. Collection of only $7 million of an estimated $1 billion of potentially improper and/or fraudulent payments clearly supports the basic point we have previously made, that fraud prevention is far more effective and less costly than detection and monitoring.[55]

Programs that favor people without insurance encourage poor decisions.

When a natural disaster strikes, people who have insurance are better off than people who do not have insurance for several reasons. First, people are eligible for federal disaster assistance only if the president officially declares an affected area to be a disaster area, but insurance covers damage regardless of a disaster declaration. Second, insurance provides better compensation than disaster assistance, covering more and better repairs to homes and paying more money for lost possessions, such as clothing, furniture, jewelry, household items, and automobiles. Third, federal assistance to individuals and households is capped at a dollar amount set by law (although people like Lawanda Williams have found ways to beat the system). Finally, much of the disaster assistance given out by the federal government comes in the form of loans that must be repaid. With a major disaster like Hurricane Katrina that disrupts a regional economy, earning the money to repay a loan can be difficult.

Nevertheless, the federal government offers disaster assistance after the fact to those who choose not to purchase insurance, and the cost to taxpayers is significant. As business professor Scott Harrington notes: "The government seems unable to withhold disaster assistance from people who fail to buy private or government insurance. Politicians enjoy exercising their charitable impulses—with taxpayers' money—and many taxpayers are sympathetic to helping disaster victims."[56]

When a homeowner has insurance, the government is able to spend less on disaster assistance to that individual homeowner or family because a person cannot receive disaster assistance for expenses that should be covered by insurance. As discussed in later chapters of this book, the federal government offers flood insurance at affordable rates so that it will spend less on disaster assistance. On the other side of the coin, the government spends more on homeowners and families who do not have insurance. For example, under the provisions of FEMA's Individuals and Households Program (IHP), non-housing-related assistance may be used to repair a damaged vehicle. If a person has purchased the more expensive "comprehensive" automobile coverage, however, the damage would be covered by the insurance policy. In this regard, IHP assistance favors the person who does not protect his or her assets through insurance.

IHP housing-related assistance provides another example of a program that is more costly to the government when it comes to people who do not have insurance. The assistance is available to people who are not required to purchase flood insurance—if they do not have a federally backed mortgage, or if they live outside of the 100-year floodplain—and have chosen not to purchase flood insurance. (In common usage, people speak of a "100-year floodplain" to describe an area that has a one percent chance of flooding each year, or once in 100 years.) For people who have flood insurance, damage caused by flooding covered by their insurance policy.

Again, the point is that the government spends more per uninsured household, but uninsured households are not necessarily better off than insured households because of it. IHP housing-related assistance is limited to making the property habitable again, while flood insurance helps the homeowner restore the property to its previous condition. To restore property to its previous condition, an uninsured homeowner must take out a low-interest loan from the Small Business Administration. It is also important to note that people who are legally required to purchase flood insurance because they live in the 100-year floodplain and/or have a federally backed mortgage, but who violate this legal obligation, are not eligible for housing-related assistance.

Nevertheless, the end result is that taxpayer money is being used to assist people who have not protected themselves. In the case of uninsured homeowners taking out low-interest loans from the SBA, taxpayers bear the costs, too. The government itself is in debt, and is borrowing money to loan it to homeowners at rates much lower than what a bank would charge. Although homeowners who have flood insurance receive much better benefits than those who forego insurance, the allocation of taxpayer money in this way seems to reward those who are less responsible. Many people decide not to purchase flood insurance because they believe that the federal government will bail them out.

Conservative columnist Michelle Malkin criticized the federal government's response to two disasters in the early 1990s—the Los Angeles earthquake and Hurricane Andrew, which struck Florida. Malkin noted that, although Andrew caused more damage than the earthquake, the government spent more on assistance in California because fewer people there had insurance to cover their losses. Malkin asked, "Why should the government reward people who fail to insure themselves? That only increases the likelihood that they will fail to buy insurance for the next big disaster."[57]

Many who question the federal government's disaster assistance policy say that disaster assistance encourages people not only to forego insurance, but also to continue to build homes in high-risk areas without taking appropriate protective measures, such as elevating a home in flood-prone areas or building stronger roofs in hurricane zones. As political science professor Donald Kettl explained, "When the federal government comes in and writes a check, you will keep doing things over and over because . . . it is how people have formed their expectations."[58]

Ironically, the prestigious magazine *Science* published a special issue on disaster relief just weeks before Hurricane Katrina hit the Gulf Coast. The focus of the issue was on international disaster relief efforts in the wake of the tsunami that killed hundreds of thousands of people in Asia at the end of 2004. In an opinion article, three risk management experts argued that the international community should help developing nations by providing funds for disaster preparation rather than disaster recovery. The article mentions numerous methods through which disaster-prevention aid—as opposed to disaster-relief aid—could help poor people in developing countries. One suggestion was to encourage them to earthquake-proof their homes or grow certain crops that would be less susceptible to weather conditions. By making "assistance contingent on requirements or incentives for prevention as part of a comprehensive risk-management program, pre-disaster assistance can reduce the human and economic toll that disasters take on the poor."[59] This is an interesting argument: One reason that many say post-Katrina relief costs were so high is that poor people were less likely to purchase insurance and were also less likely to evacuate the affected areas because they did not have transportation. Perhaps the federal government could explore similar methods of better preparing low-income families and communities for natural disasters, rather than offering more expensive post-disaster aid.

Streamlining financial assistance facilitates fraud.
Faced with widespread criticism of how it handled the evacuation and rescue efforts before and immediately after Katrina's landfall, FEMA's reaction included what many would call "throwing money at the problem." To help people with their immediate

Special Inspector General for Hurricane Katrina Recovery Act

With Congress appropriating tens of billions of dollars to the hurricane recovery effort, some legislators thought that the spending posed a special danger of fraud and waste. A group of representatives introduced the following bill, which would have required the appointment of a special investigator to monitor the recovery effort. Although this bill did not pass, Congress did include money for fraud prevention in later appropriations bills.

(1) It shall be the duty of the Special Inspector General to conduct, supervise, and coordinate audits and investigations of the treatment, handling, and expenditure of amounts appropriated or otherwise made available for Hurricane Katrina recovery by the Federal Government, and of the programs, operations, and contracts carried out utilizing such funds, including—

    (A) the oversight and accounting of the obligation and expenditure of such funds;

    (B) the monitoring and review of reconstruction activities funded by such funds;

    (C) the monitoring and review of contracts funded by such funds;

needs, FEMA gave people $2,000 checks, or debit cards that could be used anywhere that accepted debit. Through February 2006, according to FEMA statistics cited by GAO, FEMA had distributed $2.3 billion in these expedited assistance payments to individuals, or about 37 percent of the IHP aid for Katrina and Rita victims. Other financial assistance was distributed for housing expenses and home repairs. With the rapid distribution of money, however, many people obtained money to which they were not entitled. Perhaps the most egregious case uncovered by the GAO was the following:

> A convicted felon, housed in a Louisiana prison from April 2001 to the present . . . registered for IHP assistance by

(D) the monitoring and review of the transfer of such funds and associated information between and among departments, agencies, and entities of the United States, and private and nongovernmental entities; and

(E) the maintenance of records on the use of such funds to facilitate future audits and investigations of the use of such funds. . . .

(5) The Special Inspector General shall, within 10 days after the date of the appointment of the Special Inspector General, complete the following:

(A) Open a 24-hour fraud, waste, and abuse hotline.

(B) Deploy auditors and investigators to the Gulf of Mexico Region of the United States.

(C) Announce a strategic plan for oversight, including audits of no-bid contracts.

(D) Go to the Gulf of Mexico Region of the United States media with anti-fraud message.

(E) Liaise with Hurricane Katrina recovery Federal agencies to identify vulnerabilities.

(F) Coordinate interagency oversight elements through creation of a task force.

Source: H.R. 3737 (109th Congress).

telephone. The registrant made a FEMA claim using a post office box address in Louisiana as his damaged property address to qualify for IHP payments for expedited assistance, rental assistance, and personal property replacement. Two of these payments were made via checks sent to the address he falsely claimed as his current residence, and the final payment was sent via electronic funds transfer (EFT) to someone who also listed the same current address on the checking account. FEMA paid over $20,000 to the registrant even though the damaged property address on the registration was a post office box address and the registrant was incarcerated throughout the disaster period.[60]

GAO investigations of FEMA's Katrina and Rita spending also revealed the following: millions of dollars in payments to more than 100 people incarcerated in prisons at the time of the disasters; payments of $1.5 million for 750 debit cards that the agency could not verify went to hurricane victims; the use of debit cards for purchases such as diamond jewelry, an all-inclusive one-week vacation at a Caribbean resort, five season tickets for New Orleans Saints football games, a strip club bill, a $200 bottle of champagne, *Girls Gone Wild* videos, and fireworks; payments to international university students who, as non-U.S. residents, did not qualify for aid; and payments to people in the country on temporary work visas who were working in seafood processing facilities (so-called "guest workers"), who did not qualify for aid.

The unique circumstances of the 2005 hurricane season further opened the door for fraud because the president declared areas hit by hurricanes Katrina and Rita to be disaster areas. Because Rita struck before people had rebuilt from Katrina, FEMA supposedly instituted a policy to ensure that the agency did not make relief payments to the same people for both hurricanes. In fact, the agency soon disabled the mechanism for checking Rita applications against Katrina applications "in order

Above, officials prepare for Hurricane Rita evacuees on September 21, 2005, in Tyler, Texas. Following so closely on the heels of Hurricane Katrina, Rita caused destruction in many areas of Louisiana that already had seen damage.

to process disaster claims more quickly, because the manual review process that they had intended for these duplicate registrations would have held up many eligible payments."[61]

The GAO's review of payments to Katrina and Rita victims found that, as a result of disabling their cross-checking:

FEMA paid nearly $20 million in duplicate payments to individuals who submitted duplicate registrations using the same [Social Security numbers] and damaged addresses. The nearly $20 million includes duplicate payments for all areas of IHP assistance, including expedited assistance, rental assistance, housing replacement payments, or a combination of these. In five of the six cases where we performed investigative work, the same individual received duplicate payments to replace the same damaged property. The individuals also failed to provide FEMA with evidence that they had replaced the items or conducted repair work after Hurricane Katrina, only to have those items or that work destroyed again by Hurricane Rita. In all cases, FEMA performed its first physical inspection of the damaged property after the passing of both hurricanes.[62]

The most remarkable implication of this finding relates to rental assistance. FEMA offers people money to cover the cost of renting temporary housing. GAO's findings suggest that a person could be receiving two of these payments at once, even though the second storm did nothing to increase rental costs.

Although it might seem that FEMA's streamlined approach was unique due to the sheer number of people and wide area affected by Katrina and Rita, the organization's approach was nothing new, nor was criticism of the approach. Writing about FEMA's response to the 1994 Los Angeles earthquake, Michelle Malkin noted that FEMA had sent "hundreds of disaster housing checks (worth up to $3,450 each) to people whose homes are livable, some of whom say they never requested the housing assistance," because the agency simply sent checks to anyone in affected areas who inquired about any type of aid (housing or nonhousing).[63] Although the agency defended what Malkin called its "scattershot" approach by saying that only a few people called to complain that they had received money that they did not need, Malkin asked, "Is the number of calls from dissatisfied check recipients really an accurate gauge of efficiency? Perhaps the accelerated response policy made FEMA look more responsible in the short run, but in truth, it simply squandered resources that ought to have been targeted more responsibly to those in crisis."[64]

Providing multiple forms of assistance allows people to beat the system.

Direct payments to individuals are only part of the complete federal disaster relief package. In addition to payments under the IHP program that are meant to cover personal and family temporary housing costs (i.e., payments intended for an affected individual's or household's actual out-of-pocket cost of renting the housing), FEMA also provided many people with housing. For example, FEMA housed people in trailers and also provided local and state governments with funds to rent apartments to house people displaced by Katrina.

Although FEMA's multifaceted approach was probably more helpful to addressing the needs of Katrina evacuees, it also opened the door to fraud. Many people continued to receive the monetary payments meant to cover the cost of rent for months after they began living rent-free in FEMA trailers or in apartments rented with FEMA funds. In other words, although they were not paying rent, they continued to receive taxpayer money to compensate them for nonexistent rental expenses. Although some of the payments were based on fraudulent claims, FEMA officials actually reported to GAO that they

> did not believe that the initial rental assistance payment, provided to cover the first few months of rental housing, should be considered a duplication of benefits if it was provided to trailer residents. FEMA officials argued that this amount is designed to assist disaster victims in moving from temporary emergency housing into a normal apartment or home lease situation.[65]

The report found that FEMA had made rental assistance payments totaling nearly $17 million to 8,600 applicants living rent-free in FEMA-funded trailers. As to the apartments rented by local or state governments, the GAO report stated that the investigating agency could not evaluate the extent to which duplicate payments had been made because FEMA did not maintain adequate data. FEMA relied on local and state governments to provide information on the people living in FEMA-funded apartments and did not require these governments to collect information about the people living in the apartments until after they had moved in—and possibly had already moved out. FEMA also paid for people to stay in hotel rooms and did not verify that people staying in FEMA-paid hotel rooms were not also receiving rental assistance. As a result, one person received thousands of dollars in rental assistance aid while staying 70 nights at a Hawaii hotel—at a cost to taxpayers of over $8,000—even though the person was entitled to neither the money nor the hotel accommodations because the person was not living at the damaged property at the time of the disasters.

Summary

Although the process of rebuilding from Katrina and Rita will take years, and the Gulf Coast continues to request outside assistance, an examination of federal spending in the wake of the storms revealed waste and fraud. In their haste to make payments to hurricane victims, FEMA did little to verify that people requesting money had been affected by the storm and were not receiving other forms of relief. Additionally, post-disaster financial relief is a double-edged sword, in that people are less likely to responsibly prepare themselves for a future disaster.

The next chapters look at the National Flood Insurance Program, one example of a program that attempts to protect people in advance from the financial hardships associated with disaster.

The National Flood Insurance Program Must Be Maintained or Expanded

Cindy Reed of Pass Christian, Mississippi, and her brother made very different decisions when it came to buying insurance for their homes. Reed and her husband, having experienced several hurricanes while previously living in Virginia Beach, Virginia, decided to protect themselves against hurricane damage. In addition to a standard homeowner's insurance policy, they purchased a flood insurance policy backed by the National Flood Insurance Program (NFIP), established by the federal government. Because of the extensive damage that floods can cause, private insurance companies do not cover flood damage in standard homeowner's policies, and people therefore must purchase separate flood insurance. Cindy's brother, however, was more comfortable taking risks. Because he did not live in a high-risk flood zone, he decided to not purchase an additional flood insurance policy.

When Hurricane Katrina hit in 2005, Cindy Reed and her family were lucky that their home did not collapse, as many of their neighbors' homes did; however, the flood reached 13 feet up the living room walls and caused extensive damage. Fortunately for the family, the damage to their home and their lost belongings were paid for by the flood insurance they had purchased. Cindy's brother, who had just recently purchased his home and had not even made the first mortgage payment, was not so lucky. The storm completely destroyed his home, and the damage was not covered by his standard homeowner's insurance. Like many people in the Gulf Coast region, Reed's brother was left owing thousands of dollars on a home that no longer existed.

The predicament faced by Cindy Reed's brother and thousands of others was preventable. In 1968, Congress established the National Flood Insurance Program (NFIP) as a means of protecting homeowners from the devastating losses that can often be caused by flooding. Recounting the history of the program, Chad Berginnis of the Association of State Floodplain Managers noted that Congress designed the program to encourage communities and homeowners to build homes to be better protected against flood damage. He testified before Congress as it considered whether to overhaul or eliminate NFIP:

> The program was established as a "quid-pro-quo" program. Through it, relief from the impacts of flood damages in the form of federally-backed flood insurance became available to citizens in participating communities contingent on flood loss reduction measures embodied in state and local floodplain management regulations. Occupants of existing structures in flood-prone areas would benefit from subsidized flood insurance premiums, but occupants of new structures would have to pay actuarially based premiums. This was based on the concept that those already living in the floodplain did not understand the flood risk involved in their locational decisions, but future occupants would through information

provided by the NFIP—via flood studies and maps. The original program would be voluntary in terms of community participation and the purchase of flood insurance.[66]

In other words, Congress recognized that many people had already built homes in areas that were prone to flooding, and therefore offered them flood insurance at rates much lower than warranted by the flood risk. To encourage people building new homes to choose locations and design their homes with flood risks in mind, however, anyone building a new home would have to pay "actuarial rates" for flood insurance. These are rates based on the risk of flood loss, as determined by insurance officials, taking into account the likelihood of flooding and the way the house was built. Flood risk is based on flood maps that are created for communities that have chosen to participate in the program. By calculating insurance rates based on flood risk, people would have an incentive to build in areas that had a lower risk—and therefore a lower insurance rate.

During the early years of the NFIP's existence, however, too few communities decided to participate in the program, and too few people bought flood insurance. The success of any insurance program depends on the sale of a large number of policies, so that the risk of having to pay out a claim is spread out among a number of policies. If policies are purchased by only a few people who are at risk of flood loss, the likelihood is that the insurance company will need to pay out more money than it is making. Therefore, to encourage more communities to participate in the program and more individual homeowners to purchase flood insurance, Congress made some changes to the law in 1973. First, communities would have to participate in the program in order to receive any type of construction assistance from the federal government. Second, anyone who purchased a home using a mortgage (home loan) backed by the federal government—as a significant percentage of mortgages are—would have to purchase flood insurance.

The National Flood Insurance Program is self-supporting and lowers disaster relief costs.

The enormous damages caused by Hurricane Katrina, not to mention Hurricane Rita in the same year, put a great deal of financial strain on the flood insurance program. Previously, FEMA had touted the program as self-supporting. In 2004, proclaiming NFIP to be "debt-free," the director of FEMA's mitigation division, Anthony S. Lowe, explained to Congress that NFIP supports itself by selling insurance policies. In years in which losses are severe, however, the program borrows money from the federal government to pay claims. Lowe testified:

> As you know, the program does not receive appropriations to pay for its operations. It is self-supporting through premium income from our policyholders, enabling us to pay losses which are have averaged approximately $750 million per year. However, flood losses for a specific year can vary significantly from this average. When flood losses exceed NFIP reserves, we have the authority to borrow funds from the U.S. Treasury to pay for those losses. Whenever we have to borrow from the Treasury to pay for historically high losses, we must repay with interest what we borrowed. Since 1986, when the program received its last appropriation, we have borrowed and repaid approximately $2.7 billion.[67]

The huge financial strains put on NFIP by claims related to Katrina and Rita must be put into the context of the overall toll of the disaster. While authorizing more than $20 billion in loans to NFIP in the wake of the hurricanes, Congress also granted more than four times that amount in direct financial assistance to hurricane victims, as well as passing tax relief packages also running into the billions of dollars. Supporters of NFIP note that one of the original intents of the program was to reduce the costs of disaster relief borne by the federal government. Without NFIP, the federal government might have spent even more on relief.

A report by the Congressional Research Service strongly suggested that the NFIP spared the government from bailing out homeowners who had flood insurance, as they did with those homeowners who did not have flood insurance. The report acknowledged a "national debate as to whether the federal government should pay for catastrophe losses that are not covered by insurance either because the damage was caused by excluded perils, or because the insurance has become insolvent, or because the persons or entities suffering the losses were not insured." However, the report also pointed out that the government's multibillion-dollar aid package included:

> $11.9 billion for Community Development Block Grants to address the uninsured flood loss problem. The grants would be used to address the needs of homeowners. Funds will be allocated, in grants of up to $150,000, to certain eligible homeowners whose primary residences were destroyed or severely damaged following Hurricanes Katrina and Rita.[68]

If the alternative to a federally supported flood insurance program (which at least collects premiums) is simply making payments after the fact to people who have not purchased insurance, supporters of NFIP say that federal loans to the program to keep it operating are worthwhile. As Chad Berginnis, of the Association of State Floodplain Managers, asserted: "Between 1978 and the end of 2004, the NFIP has paid $13.7 billion in losses that would otherwise have been paid by taxpayers through disaster assistance or borne by home and business owners themselves."[69]

Even before Katrina, Congress had sought to strengthen the financial footing of NFIP. The passage of the Flood Insurance Reform Act of 2004 enabled FEMA to stem losses related to properties that had flooded repeatedly. Among other tools, the law enabled FEMA to reduce costs associated with "repetitive loss properties" by (1) enabling FEMA to pay to "mitigate" these properties, meaning to reduce the risk of flood through raising the home or other construction methods; (2) allowing NFIP to drastically raise the cost of insurance for homeowners who refuse to allow FEMA to mitigate the property; and (3) by allowing FEMA to purchase properties that are subject to great flood risk.

The availability of flood insurance allows people to build homes in desirable areas.

Steven Feldmann, the director of community affairs for a home-builder in suburban Cincinnati, testified before Congress on behalf of the National Association of Home Builders that the NFIP is essential to community development. "The availability and the affordability of flood insurance give homebuyers and homeowners the opportunity to live in a home of their choice in a location of their choice, even when the home lies within a floodplain," he told a Senate subcommittee.[70]

Although building in a "floodplain" might not sound like a good idea, the reality is that millions of people live in areas prone to flooding. NFIP divides communities into "flood zones," some of which have a minimal risk of flooding, and others that are almost certain to flood. For a typical homeowner with a 30-year mortgage, buying or building a home in a 100-year floodplain means that the chance of flooding is greater than 1 in 4 during the life of the 30-year mortgage. Officially, NFIP designates these areas as "Zone A" flood zones, and the federal government requires homeowners in these areas to purchase flood insurance in order to qualify for a federally backed mortgage. With the risk of flooding so high, the government does not want to lend money to a homeowner in a Zone A location without flood insurance, out of fear that the lender will not repay the loan if the house is destroyed by flood.

According to Feldmann, allowing homeowners to build in areas of their choice, even if the risk of flooding is elevated, allows the development of communities based on personal preferences, such as the desire to live near water. He testified:

The choices American consumers make when they are buying homes are some of the most critical aspects of the home buying process. Through decisions about where to live, where to shop and how to get around town, consumers apply the power of the marketplace to shape the nation's communities. The NFIP, by enabling the choice of purchasing a home in a floodplain, allows consumer preferences to shape towns and cities into communities that maximize quality of life and economic development.[71]

Further, argued Feldmann, the desire to build in flood-prone areas is a matter of necessity rather than choice for many communities. Banishing building from these areas would mean that less land would be available for building, and the reduction in supply would inevitably result in an increase in price for land on which houses could be built. If NFIP were to be eliminated, testified Feldmann:

> Many communities would be unable to provide affordable housing to many of their citizens. Despite a decade of unprecedented prosperity, many communities are seeing a growing gap between the supply and demand for housing. Families across the economic spectrum are finding it increasingly difficult to find a home that meets their needs. One of the leading causes of the housing affordability problem is the shortage of buildable land. By guaranteeing affordable flood insurance, the NFIP allows communities to use land that would otherwise be too costly due to high flood insurance premiums. Through the NFIP, flood insurance policies remain available and affordable and residential structures can be constructed in floodplains as long as they are built to withstand flooding. Therefore the NFIP provides the means by which communities can address housing needs by making homeownership in areas prone to flooding safe, affordable and practical.[72]

National Flood Insurance Act

(a) Necessity and reasons for flood insurance program
The Congress finds that

(1) from time to time flood disasters have created personal hardships and economic distress which have required unforeseen disaster relief measures and have placed an increasing burden on the Nation's resources;

(2) despite the installation of preventive and protective works and the adoption of other public programs designed to reduce losses caused by flood damage, these methods have not been sufficient to protect adequately against growing exposure to future flood losses;

(3) as a matter of national policy, a reasonable method of sharing the risk of flood losses is through a program of flood insurance which can complement and encourage preventive and protective measures; and

(4) if such a program is initiated and carried out gradually, it can be expanded as knowledge is gained and experience is appraised, thus eventually making flood insurance coverage available on reasonable terms and conditions to persons who have need for such protection.

(b) Participation of Federal Government in flood insurance program carried out by private insurance industry
The Congress also finds that

(1) many factors have made it uneconomic for the private insurance industry alone to make flood insurance available to those in need of such protection on reasonable terms and conditions; but

(2) a program of flood insurance with large-scale participation of the Federal Government and carried out to the maximum extent practicable by the private insurance industry is feasible and can be initiated.

(c) Unified national program for flood plain management
The Congress further finds that

(1) a program of flood insurance can promote the public interest by providing appropriate protection against the perils of flood losses and encouraging sound land use by minimizing exposure of property to flood losses; and

(2) the objectives of a flood insurance program should be integrally related to a unified national program for flood plain management and, to this end,

it is the sense of Congress that within two years following the effective date of this chapter the President should transmit to the Congress for its consideration any further proposals necessary for such a unified program, including proposals for the allocation of costs among beneficiaries of flood protection.

(d) Authorization of flood insurance program; flexibility in program

It is therefore the purpose of this chapter to

(1) authorize a flood insurance program by means of which flood insurance, over a period of time, can be made available on a nationwide basis through the cooperative efforts of the Federal Government and the private insurance industry, and

(2) provide flexibility in the program so that such flood insurance may be based on workable methods of pooling risks, minimizing costs, and distributing burdens equitably among those who will be protected by flood insurance and the general public.

(e) Land use adjustments by State and local governments; development of proposed future construction; assistance of lending and credit institutions; relation of Federal assistance to all flood-related programs; continuing studies

It is the further purpose of this chapter to

(1) encourage State and local governments to make appropriate land use adjustments to constrict the development of land which is exposed to flood damage and minimize damage caused by flood losses,

(2) guide the development of proposed future construction, where practicable, away from locations which are threatened by flood hazards,

(3) encourage lending and credit institutions, as a matter of national policy, to assist in furthering the objectives of the flood insurance program,

(4) assure that any Federal assistance provided under the program will be related closely to all flood-related programs and activities of the Federal Government, and

(5) authorize continuing studies of flood hazards in order to provide for a constant reappraisal of the flood insurance program and its effect on land use requirements.

Source: 42 U.S.C., section 4001.

In addition to the important benefit to homeowners, Feldmann also discussed the importance of NFIP to the homebuilding industry, an industry that is increasingly important to the national economy as more manufactured goods are imported. "The homebuilding industry depends upon the NFIP to be annually predictable, universally available, and fiscally viable,"[73] Feldmann said.

Broadening mandatory participation would strengthen NFIP.

Despite all of the incentives that Congress has established to encourage people to buy flood insurance, not everyone buys or maintains flood insurance. Only people who use a federally backed mortgage to buy a home located in a high-risk flood zone (i.e., having a one percent annual chance of flooding) are required to purchase flood insurance. People in lower risk zones do not have to purchase this insurance. Even in high-risk zones, many people are not subject to the law's requirement: Some people buy homes using a mortgage not backed by the federal government. Others do not have a mortgage at all—for instance, if they paid cash value for the house or inherited the house; some may have already paid off the mortgage.

Even people who are required by law to maintain flood insurance do not always maintain the required coverage. Although the government has improved measures to ensure that brokers who sell federally backed mortgages require homeowners to obtain and maintain flood insurance, a 2006 study by the RAND Corporation estimated that, nationwide, 75 to 80 percent of homeowners required by law to have flood insurance actually have it. This suggests that most people purchase flood insurance when they buy their homes, but many allow the policies to lapse at some point during the life of the mortgage.[74]

As has been discussed, many people who could benefit from flood insurance do not have it. More significantly, say supporters of NFIP, too few people are paying into the system. The RAND study examined participation rates in the NFIP and private flood insurance programs and found that, nationwide, of the approximately 3.6 million single-family homes in high-risk flood zones, only about 49 percent participated in NFIP, and only an additional 1 to 2 percent of the homes had private flood insurance. Outside of the high-risk flood zones—although flooding there is possible and is not covered by homeowner's insurance policies—only about 1 percent of single-family homes were covered by flood insurance. As a result of the relatively low percentage of at-risk homeowners who carry flood insurance, NFIP has less revenue from selling policies and is less able to support itself in the case of large-scale disasters such as Hurricane Katrina.

Proposals to increase the number of people participating in NFIP fall into three main categories: strengthening enforcement of the current requirements, extending the requirements to people living in less flood-prone areas, and requiring people with non-federally-backed mortgages to purchase flood insurance.

Like Cindy Reed's brother, who lost his home in Hurricane Katrina, many people who live outside of high-risk flood zones do not buy flood insurance because they think that they do not need it. Although the risk is smaller, the damage from a major flood can be just as severe, and homeowners in lower-risk areas can purchase flood insurance at much lower rates. Various proposals have been made to increase participation requirements.

Pamela Mayer Pogue, a state floodplain manager for Rhode Island, testified before Congress about extending the mandatory purchase requirement for people with federally backed mortgages to homes located in a 500-year floodplain (areas with a 0.2 annual percent chance of flooding). She argued that people living in 500-year floodplains have a false sense of security that causes them to reject the purchase of flood insurance. Making the purchase of flood insurance mandatory would help "in the event of other catastrophic events," she said, because "one of the lessons learned post-Katrina was that there were many flooded properties that did not have flood insurance and whose property did not fall into a 1 percent chance floodplain based on FEMA's

Flood Insurance Rate Maps (FIRMs)."[75] Although many industries, such as the homebuilding, realty, and mortgage lending industries, argue against the extension of mandatory coverage because it hampers home ownership by raising costs, Pogue testified, "It is our belief that the rates of flood insurance policies

Flood Insurance Reform Act of 2004

In 2004, before hurricanes Katrina and Rita struck the Gulf Coast, Congress sought to financially bolster the National Flood Insurance Program by allowing it to deal with properties that resulted in losses to the system.

Congress finds that—

(2) the national flood insurance program insures approximately 4,400,000 policyholders;

(3) approximately 48,000 properties currently insured under the program have experienced, within a 10-year period, 2 or more flood losses where each such loss exceeds the amount $1,000;

(4) approximately 10,000 of these repetitive-loss properties have experienced either 2 or 3 losses that cumulatively exceed building value or 4 or more losses, each exceeding $1,000;

(5) repetitive-loss properties constitute a significant drain on the resources of the national flood insurance program, costing about $200,000,000 annually;

(6) repetitive-loss properties comprise approximately 1 percent of currently insured properties but are expected to account for 25 to 30 percent of claims losses ...

(9) mitigation of repetitive-loss properties through buyouts, elevations, relocations, or flood-proofing will produce savings for policyholders under the program and for Federal taxpayers through reduced flood insurance losses and reduced Federal disaster assistance; [and]

(10) a strategy of making mitigation offers aimed at high-priority repetitive-loss properties and shifting more of the burden of recovery costs to property owners who choose to remain vulnerable to repetitive flood damage can encourage property owners to take appropriate actions that

in these areas would be reflective of the lower probability that a flood would occur and would be in line with FEMA's current preferred risk policy ... [ranging] from $112 to $317 a year."[76]

Interestingly, Chad Berginnis of the Association of State Floodplain Managers pointed out that people living in areas

reduce loss of life and property damage and benefit the financial soundness of the program....

The Director [of FEMA] may, subject to the limitations of this section, provide financial assistance to States and communities that decide to participate in the pilot program established under this section for taking actions with respect to severe repetitive loss properties ... to mitigate flood damage to such properties and losses to the National Flood Insurance Fund from such properties....

(c) Eligible Activities.—Amounts provided under this section to a State or community may be used only for the following activities:

(1) Mitigation activities.—To carry out mitigation activities that reduce flood damages to severe repetitive loss properties, including elevation, relocation, demolition, and floodproofing of structures, and minor physical localized flood control projects, and the demolition and rebuilding of properties to at least Base Flood Elevation or greater, if required by any local ordinance.

(2) Purchase.—To purchase severe repetitive loss properties....

(h) Increased Premiums in Cases of Refusal To Mitigate.—

(1) In general.—In any case in which the owner of a severe repetitive loss property refuses an offer to take action under paragraph (1) or (2) of subsection (c) with respect to such property ... thereafter the chargeable premium rate with respect to the property shall be the amount equal to 150 percent of the chargeable rate for the property at the time that the offer was made, as adjusted by any other premium adjustments otherwise applicable to the property.

Source: Pub. L. 108-264

presumably protected by levees—such as New Orleans—are not required to purchase flood insurance if the levees reduce the annual risk of flooding to less than one percent. He testified:

> The ASFPM has long advocated the concept of mandatory "residual risk" flood insurance requirements for areas behind levees and floodwalls and below dams. The cost of such a policy would be commensurate with the lower risk of flooding, yet the property owner, states, communities, and the U.S. taxpayer won't be faced with bearing the costs of a catastrophic failure.[77]

Congress debated the increase in the NFIP's borrowing authority several times, all while gradually increasing the program's borrowing authority to more than $20 billion. Many supported tying these increases to a stipulation that more people be required to purchase flood insurance. Such proposals were killed by strong opposition from realtors, mortgage lenders, and homebuilders, who argued that the requirements would harm potential homebuyers. Of course, anything that harms homebuyers would also cut into those industries' profits, but championing the "American dream" of homeownership is a politically palatable argument.

Without a federal program, homeowners would be at great risk.

NFIP exists because very few private insurance companies are willing to provide flood insurance to homeowners. With standard homeowners' policies excluding flood damage, homeowners would be at great risk if NFIP were to fail.

Congress created NFIP in 1968 as a solution to the absence of private insurance and the pressing need to protect homeowners from flood damage. In the past, the federal government has recognized that protecting people in flood-prone areas is an important national interest. The Flood Control Act of 1936 focused on protecting areas located near "navigational waters and their tributaries."[78] Rivers and other waterways have historically played an extremely important role in the transportation of goods, with many major cities having developed around major waterways such as the Mississippi River. Although the areas around rivers were indeed prone to flooding, their development as commercial and residential centers was justified by the proximity of navigable waterways.

The Mississippi River floods in the 1920s and 1930s drove private insurance companies away from the flood insurance business. According to a Congressional Research Service Report:

> During the late 1920s several dozen fire insurers sold flood insurance, but due to extreme riverine flood disasters during 1927 and 1928 in nearly all parts of the United States, all of these insurers withdrew from the market. From the late 1920s until today, flood insurance has not been considered profitable.[79]

Today, inland ports are perhaps less significant to commerce, but the historical development of cities around water has shaped where people have chosen to live and develop businesses. Thus, flood insurance remains important. Regina Lowrie, president of Gateway Funding Diversified Mortgage, a mortgage lending company, testified to Congress on behalf of the Mortgage Bankers Association:

> Over the years, the nationwide availability of affordable flood insurance has been important to expanding homeownership and building communities. The [NFIP] serves a very important function in the mortgage lending industry as it reduces the overall cost of financing a property located in a flood prone area by providing affordable and reliable flood insurance. . . . Without a reliable and uninterrupted source of flood insurance, we believe mortgage credit would, at best, be more expensive, or at worst, unavailable in many markets.[80]

Summary

Hurricanes Katrina and Rita created severe financial difficulties for the National Flood Insurance Program, which has had to borrow more than $20 billion from the federal government in order to pay claims. Supporters of the federal program say that it helps the nation because it generally supports itself and only borrows from the treasury, therefore keeping taxpayers from having to pay money to people whose homes are damaged or destroyed by flooding. Without the program, homeowners would be forced to assume the risk of flood damage because private insurance companies have, since the 1920s, generally been unwilling to offer flood insurance. People would also be less willing to build homes in areas subject to periodic flooding, harming regional economies.

Recognizing that the NFIP is deeply in debt, supporters have offered proposals to strengthen the program. Even before Katrina, Congress strengthened the program by enabling FEMA to rebuild or buy properties that had flooded repeatedly and to raise insurance premiums for homeowners who rejected such offers. Many feel that the best way to ensure the future of NFIP is to require more people to purchase flood insurance, including people who live in areas protected by levees and people who live in 500-year floodplains. Although people in lower-risk areas would pay much lower rates, their contributions to the program would help to sustain affordable flood insurance for every American who needs it.

The National Flood Insurance Program Must Be Reformed or Eliminated

Journalist John Stossel has made a career of provocative news stories. One of his favorite targets is wasteful government spending of taxpayer money to the benefit of special interest groups. Ironically, one of his better-known targets is a costly government program that often benefits wealthy people—including Stossel himself. When Stossel's beach house was destroyed by a storm in 1995, the National Flood Insurance Program covered his losses.

In a story for *Reason* magazine, a publication dedicated to libertarian and free-market principles, Stossel confessed to being a "welfare queen"—a reference used by Ronald Reagan to attack those who abused government assistance programs. He recalled that, when he first considered building a beach house, he realized the enormous risk that flooding posed to the house: "It was an absurd place to build, right on the edge of the ocean. All that stood between my house and ruin was a hundred feet of sand."[81] Nevertheless, he decided to build the house so that he and his guests could enjoy the view of the Atlantic Ocean. His reason was that he could purchase flood insurance through the government-sponsored National Flood Insurance Program for several hundred dollars per year. As his architect said when Stossel was considering whether to build: "If the ocean destroys your house, the government will pay for a new one."[82]

Allowing the flood insurance program to borrow repeatedly from the treasury costs taxpayers enormously.

Supporters of the NFIP argue that, prior to the massive losses caused by Katrina, the program was self-supporting; the income from premiums covered the cost of claims. In 1986, the structure of NFIP changed. It went from a system in which the government appropriated funds directly to the program, to one in which the program would rely on premiums to cover its expenses, though it would be able to borrow money from the U.S. Treasury when expenses exceeded its financial assets.

The ability to borrow money from the treasury to pay claims has become an enormous benefit to the program. Most insurance in the United States is provided by private insurance companies that do not have the luxury of being able to borrow from the government when they need to pay claims. Instead, they typically rely on a strategy called reinsurance, which means that the insurance company buys its own insurance for the policies it sells. Reinsurance is a complicated business, but a simple example follows: For a homeowner, the cost of replacing a house if it is destroyed by fire is too great to risk having to pay for it out of pocket, so the homeowner buys an insurance policy. If the house burns down, the insurance company pays to rebuild it. Replacing a single house is no big deal for an insurance company with thousands of policyholders, but what if a wildfire destroys an entire housing subdivision? For the insurance company, that risk is too great, so it buys reinsurance, typically in smaller amounts from numerous companies.

When Hurricane Katrina hit, NFIP fell back not on reinsurance, but on the U.S. Treasury. Before Katrina, NFIP was authorized to borrow $1.5 billion to pay claims. After Katrina, Congress extended that amount to $18.5 billion. The United States has a massive debt of its own, upon which it pays a staggering amount of interest. So, each time the federal government lends money to NFIP, it is basically lending borrowed money. Donald Marron, acting director of the Congressional Budget Office, which monitors federal spending, estimated that NFIP has been collecting only 60 percent of the premiums that it should be collecting, and that this failure costs taxpayers approximately $1.3 billion per year.[83]

In theory, NFIP is supposed to repay the treasury with interest on the money that it borrows. Many critics are skeptical that the billions borrowed to pay Katrina-related claims will ever be repaid. FEMA's director estimated that interest alone on the money borrowed to pay Katrina claims would be about $670 million in the first year. Noting this, David John of the Heritage Foundation told a Senate committee, "If interest alone eats up almost 35 percent of NFIP's annual income of roughly $2 billion, the only way that repayment is possible will be if premium income is greatly increased and average claims remain at the pre-Katrina level."[84] John expressed doubt that repayment would be feasible in the future:

> [Realistically], the only way to get these loans off of NFIP's books will be for Congress eventually to forgive them. . . . While losses from a single storm like Hurricane Katrina may be exceptional, scientists expect hurricane activity to build in coming years. As millions of Americans continue to relocate to flood-prone areas and property values in those areas continue to rise, NFIP can expect to face much higher levels of annual claims then it has in the past. Unless premiums income

grows at least as fast, the program's request for increased borrowing authority is likely to be an annual event rather than an exception caused by a catastrophe.[85]

THE LETTER OF THE LAW

Increased Borrowing Authority for NFIP

When hurricanes Katrina and Rita hit, many people made legitimate claims on their flood insurance policies, but the program did not have the money to pay these claims. Members of Congress voted on several occasions to increase the program's ability to borrow money from the federal government, increasing the amount from $1.5 billion to nearly $21 billion.

SEC. 2. INCREASE IN BORROWING AUTHORITY.
The first sentence of subsection (a) of section 1309 of the National Flood Insurance Act of 1968 (42 U.S.C. 4016(a)) is amended by inserting before the period at the end the following: '; except that, through September 30, 2008, clause (2) of this sentence shall be applied by substituting '$3,500,000,000' for '$1,500,000,000'.

Source: Public Law No: 109-65 (2005)

SEC. 2. INCREASE IN BORROWING AUTHORITY.
The first sentence of subsection (a) of section 1309 of the National Flood Insurance Act of 1968 (42 U.S.C. 4016(a)), as amended by the National Flood Insurance Program Enhanced Borrowing Authority Act of 2005 (Public Law 109-65; 119 Stat. 1998), is amended by striking '$3,500,000,000' and inserting '$18,500,000,000'.

Source: Public Law No: 109-106 (2005)

SEC. 2. INCREASE IN BORROWING AUTHORITY.
The first sentence of subsection (a) of section 1309 of the National Flood Insurance Act of 1968 (42 U.S.C. 4016(a)), as amended by the National Flood Insurance Program Further Enhanced Borrowing Authority Act of 2005 (Public Law 109-106; 119 Stat. 2288), is amended by striking "$18,500,000,000" and inserting "$20,775,000,000".

Source: Public Law No: 109-208 (2006)

Supporters of NFIP suggest that, although federal loans to NFIP do result in significant costs to the treasury, the costs are more than made up for by reducing the amount of money paid in disaster relief. This is based on the theory that people who have flood insurance are less likely to need financial assistance to rebuild their homes.

Opponents of federally subsidized flood insurance question whether direct financial assistance to flood victims and flood insurance can coexist. As real estate professor Carolyn Dehring points out in *Regulation* magazine, "Arguments that ex-ante [beforehand] subsidies are less costly than ex-post [after the fact] disaster aid fail to account for how the implicit promise of assistance from the U.S. government affects consumer decisions to insure."[86] In other words, why would someone buy flood insurance if he or she believes that the government will help to rebuild if a catastrophe strikes, whether or not the policy was purchased?

Business professor Scott Harrington notes that federal expenditures on disaster relief "could be reduced if people who failed to buy insurance were to forfeit their eligibility for disaster assistance," but admits that such a solution is unlikely in the current political climate.[87]

The flood insurance program encourages unwise decisions.

When John Stossel built his beach home, he knew that he was doing something risky. Unlike other risky decisions that investors might make, such as buying stock in an unproven company, Stossel had little to fear in deciding to invest in a beachfront home, because the availability of low-cost insurance made it possible to build a house on the beach without worrying about the flood risk adding costs to the project. Some economists say that government subsidies for flood insurance create a "moral hazard," meaning that people will behave inappropriately if they do not bear the full consequences of their actions.

Normally, the cost of insurance is based on risk. For example, insurance companies determine that teenage drivers are much more likely to have accidents than middle-aged adults. Similarly, people who have received speeding or other traffic tickets are also more likely to have accidents, as are people who drive certain types of vehicles, such as high-powered sports cars. In order to reduce the costs that they pay for insurance, people are often willing to adjust their behavior. For example, a parent might not buy a teenager his or her own car, but instead allow the teen to drive a parent's car on limited occasions, which results in a much lower insurance rate. Although the government regulates insurance rates, particularly at the state level, it does not typically subsidize insurance, and therefore people must weigh the costs associated with risky behavior against the benefits of stopping that behavior.

An additional problem is that a program encouraging building in flood-prone areas benefits people who do not need financial assistance from the government, including people who build luxury homes, vacation homes, or beach houses to rent out as a money-making venture. Paul Gessing of the National Taxpayers Union, which battles government waste, brought up Stossel's story as he asked Congress to overhaul NFIP:

> Asking U.S. taxpayers to spend billions annually on government programs and revenue transfers designed with the purpose of assisting poor and lower-income Americans is one thing; but asking them to spend additional billions on the NFIP, which is more of a taxpayer-financed "safety net" for millionaires, is yet another. It is after all predominantly wealthy people with enough disposable income to own beachfront property who choose to live or have a second home in risky areas. Then, because it is priced far below market value, flood insurance proves even more attractive to wealthy homeowners who know a good deal when they see it.

Thus, the wealthy snap up coverage while the poor are often left unprotected when disaster strikes.[88]

Recent changes do not go far enough.

Congress has gradually reduced the degree to which the government subsidizes flood insurance. For example, the Flood Insurance Reform Act of 2004 enabled FEMA to minimize expenditures on properties upon which multiple flood insurance claims had been made by enabling the agency to either purchase the property at a fair price or pay for improvements that would limit future flood damages. The law also required the NFIP to charge homeowners nonsubsidized, market-rate premiums for properties built after 1974 or after flood maps became available for the area.

The Flood Insurance Reform Act was intended to result in savings to the program, but the reforms perpetuated the practice of subsidizing high-risk properties at taxpayers' expense. First, private insurers would not being willing to purchase or pay for improvements to properties upon which they have already paid multiple claims. They would simply drop coverage or charge higher rates. Second, not all homes are covered by the requirement to charge market-rate premiums.

Supporters of NFIP argue that the continuation of subsidies is necessary because private insurers had been dropping out of the flood insurance business when NFIP was established in 1968. Some NFIP supporters, however, blame consumers rather than the insurance companies for the lack of flood insurance. Real estate professor Carolyn Dehring writes that people who justify the subsidized program based on the lack of private insurance options ignore "the fact that consumers are unwilling to pay premiums that cover loss exposure, and the difficulty in spreading risk over both high and low risk consumers because lower risk consumers will not purchase at the pooled rate."[89] In other words, people are simply not willing to pay the cost of insurance. In other types of insurance markets, such as life insurance, however, the government is not willing to provide low-cost insurance to people who do not want to pay full price.

Many critics of the National Flood Insurance Program concede that the program has become so entrenched that it would be difficult for Congress to privatize the flood insurance market by ending the NFIP. Some recent proposals to make NFIP more financially sound include eliminating the premium subsidies for structures built prior to the availability of an NFIP flood map,[90] or eliminating the premium subsidies only on those older properties worth more than a certain amount;[91] eliminating premium subsidies for properties on which more than one damage claim has been made;[92] and charging higher premiums for vacation homes or beach-rental houses.[93]

Some supporters of flood insurance reform believe that privatizing the flood insurance business would be possible. Supporters of a free-market solution found an unlikely ally in Robert Hunter of the Consumer Federation of America, an organization that typically supports heavy regulation of industries to protect consumers. Hunter helped to build the NFIP as its administrator during the 1970s. He testified before Congress, "I love the National Flood Insurance Program. I poured 10 years of my life into getting it started. . . . [However,] I must sadly raise the question of whether the flood insurance program should be ended."[94] Hunter suggested that today, insurers might be more willing to enter the flood insurance market if it were privatized because new technology and updated flood maps allow insurers to more accurately judge flood risk and set premiums that cover the risk.

Indeed, in June 2006, Fireman's Fund announced that it was entering the flood insurance market, offering a policy with payouts higher than NFIP's $250,000 for structural damage and $100,000 for personal property. Unlike NFIP, Fireman's Fund also offered flood coverage for finished basements. Appealing to the high-end homeowner, Bob Courtemanche, president of Fireman's Fund Personal Insurance, said,

The limitations of an NFIP policy may not be sufficient for today's finest homes. In addition to providing more than adequate excess coverage over and above NFIP, no other insurer offers flood coverage as complete in terms of property covered, limits or possible flood zone locations as Fireman's Fund.[95]

Noting the irony that his group, generally so opposed to government regulation, would agree so heartily with the Consumer Federation of America, Gessing testified that the free market should be allowed to resolve the question of whether privatizing flood insurance would work:

> If, after the marketplace is free of federal subsidies that have kept for-profit firms out of the business, private companies remain skeptical of the profitability of providing flood insurance, all is still not lost. That reaction may be yet another tool to reinforce the message that living in flood-prone areas is risky and that people should be forced to bear the costs of such an unwise move.[96]

Private insurers can take advantage of the flood exclusion.

During Katrina, New Orleans was battered by strong winds and heavy rain, followed by a surge of floodwater as the levees failed and the bowl-shaped city filled with water. A hurricane of Katrina's magnitude causes enormous amounts of damage through wind alone, ripping roofs from houses, shattering glass, and blowing debris through the air. When this wind is followed by a flood that fills a house with water, the damage is compounded. For the purposes of filing insurance claims, a storm leaves the important question of which damages were caused by wind and which damages were caused by the flood. The reason for this question's importance, of course, is that, under the current system of insurance, private insurers sell homeowner's policies that exclude flood damage. Thus, the insurance company

FROM THE BENCH

Louisiana Judge Rules that Homeowners' Policies Cover Damage from Levee Breach

After Hurricane Katrina, certain homeowners and New Orleans' Xavier University sued their insurance companies, claiming that the insurance companies should cover damages under policies that excluded flood damage. The property owners argued that the term "flood" did not clearly include damage caused by the collapse of New Orleans's levees. The trial judge agreed with the property owners and refused to dismiss the case:

> The salient question becomes whether, in the context of an all-risk policy where coverage is provided for direct loss to property, these insurance provisions which exclude coverage for water damage caused by "flood" clearly and unambiguously exclude from coverage damages caused by the alleged third party negligence of [the Orleans Levee District,] which plaintiffs contend caused a section of the floodwall at the 17th Street Canal to break causing water to enter the streets of the City of New Orleans and homes of the plaintiffs in this suit. While words and phrases in insurance polices are to be construed using their plain, ordinary and generally prevailing meaning, unless the words have acquired a technical meaning, an ambiguity arises where a term is susceptible to two reasonable interpretations.... Simply put, the question before the court is whether it is reasonable to find in the absence of further definition or provision in the [Insurance Service Office (ISO)] policy that there are two interpretations of the term "flood"—one which encompasses both a "flood" which occurs solely because of natural causes and a "flood" which occurs because of the negligent or intentional act of man and one which limits itself only to a flood which occurs solely because of natural causes....
>
> Insurers also argue that the existence of the National Flood Insurance Program ("NFIP") demonstrates that these policies are not meant to cover flooding of any sort. The existence and scope of the NFIP has no bearing on the rules of contractual interpretation that this Court must apply as to whether an exclusion in a policy is ambiguous....
>
> The Court finds that the ISO exclusions as contained in the Standard Fire Policies ... are ambiguous and as such the Court finds that the motion to dismiss based on the Water Exclusion must be denied....

Source: *In re Katrina Levee Breaches Consolidated Litigation*, No. 05-4182 (E.D. La., Nov. 27, 2006).

has an interest in showing that as much damage as possible was caused by flooding, thereby relieving it of responsibility for paying for those damages.

Robert Hunter of the Consumer Federation of America urged Congress to become involved in protecting NFIP from aggressive efforts by private insurance companies to attribute to flooding all or a large percentage of the damages caused by Katrina. He warned: "The more lax the federal government is in demanding that the allocation be fair to taxpayers, the more likely it is that persons without flood insurance will receive unfair or no compensation under their wind policies." [97] Hunter called upon the Government Accountability Office to investigate the claims payments of insurance companies that exclude flood damage.

Summary

Critics of the National Flood Insurance Program say that the program is a waste of taxpayer money. Because many people pay premiums that do not reflect the flood risk to their property, including owners of luxury vacation homes, critics call NFIP welfare for the rich. Additionally, many people who need flood insurance do not choose to buy it because they believe that the government will pay for the damage whether or not they have insurance. Furthermore, private insurance companies are quick to pass responsibility for damage off to the federally funded program. Many believe that further reform is needed so that people living in flood-prone areas can get reliable coverage but not at the taxpayers' expense.

Future Directions in Disaster Relief

Already strapped by Katrina and Rita relief efforts, the nation received no reprieve from natural disasters in the year following the catastrophes. When strong storms and wind caused extensive flooding in three Ohio counties near Lake Erie, the federal government responded as usual, providing emergency relief funds and loans to those who needed assistance rebuilding their homes. Perhaps fearing that the federal government was running out of relief funds, Ohio residents applied for relief at lower levels than expected, prompting federal and state officials to encourage those affected by the flood to apply for relief. "Don't hesitate to apply for the assistance you may need. The federal government has allocated sufficient funds for all those in the affected counties of Ashtabula, Geauga, and Lake who have eligible losses,"[98] FEMA's Jesse Munoz told the press. State emergency management official Nancy Dragani added, "There is enough help to go around for all who are eligible. The amounts distributed to one individual will in no way affect what disaster assistance is available to your neighbor or other eligible citizens of Ohio."[99]

Although no disasters on the order of Katrina and Rita occurred in 2006, President Bush declared more disaster areas than he did in 2005. The states in which federal disaster areas were declared in 2006, and in which residents were thus eligible for disaster relief, were: Alaska, Arizona, Arkansas, California, Delaware, Hawaii, Idaho, Illinois, Indiana, Kansas, Louisiana, Maine, Maryland, Massachusetts, Minnesota, Missouri, Nebraska, Nevada, New Hampshire, New Jersey, New Mexico, New York, North Dakota, Ohio, Oklahom, Oregon, Pennsylvania, South Carolina, South Dakota, Tennessee, Texas, Virginia, and Washington. In all, the president declared 52 disasters.

Since Katrina and Rita, much of the controversy regarding disaster assistance has necessarily been shaped by the government's response to the 2005 hurricanes. But many people are already talking about the "next big one"—what will happen if a catastrophe on the order of the 2005 hurricanes strikes again soon. With the National Flood Insurance Program already in a $23 billion hole, some wonder if the program could survive another major blow. Many people suggest that global warming caused by pollution will only make hurricane seasons more destructive in the future. With the nation facing the prospect of mounting losses of life and property, and insurance companies pulling out of markets in Florida and other hurricane-prone states, some have proposed a national insurance system that covers all disasters, not just flooding. These controversies will drive debate for years to come.

Can the National Flood Insurance Program Withstand Another Major Disaster?

One result of the devastation caused by hurricanes Katrina and Rita is that more Americans bought flood insurance. FEMA announced that sales of NFIP policies rose 13 percent from

November 2005 to November 2006, with increases as high as 81 percent in Mississippi. Of course, agreeing to carry flood insurance is a condition of some forms of federal disaster assistance, so that requirement undoubtedly had an impact on Mississippi's

Legislative Proposals for Disaster Insurance: HIAA

Members of Congress have proposed different approaches to ensuring that consumers have access to homeowner's and renter's insurance by providing federal support for coverage of disasters such as hurricanes and earthquakes. The Homeowners' Insurance Availability Act of 2007 (HIAA) calls for using federal funding to create a "reinsurance" program that allows insurance companies to cover their risks related to natural disasters. An excerpt follows:

Homeowners' Insurance Availability Act of 2007
  (a) In General- The Secretary of the Treasury shall carry out a program under this Act to make reinsurance coverage available through contracts for reinsurance coverage under section 5, which shall be made available for purchase by purchasers under section 5(a)(1) only through auctions under section 5(a).
  (b) Purpose- The program shall be designed to make reinsurance coverage under this Act available to improve the availability of homeowners' insurance for the purpose of facilitating the pooling, and spreading the risk, of catastrophic financial losses from disasters and to improve the solvency of homeowners' insurance markets.
  (c) Contract Principles- Under the program under this Act, the Secretary shall offer reinsurance coverage through contracts with covered purchasers, which contracts—
    (1) shall not displace or compete with the private insurance or reinsurance markets or capital markets;
    (2) shall minimize the administrative costs of the Federal Government; and
    (3) shall provide coverage based solely on insured losses within the region established pursuant to section 5(a) for which the auction is held.

Source: H.R. 330 (110th Congress).

increases. However, many states far from the hurricane-hit area saw double-digit increases, too.

Part of the reason for the increase, one insurance expert told the Associated Press, is that national media coverage of hurricanes Katrina and Rita brought to people's attention the fact that homeowner's policies do not cover flood damage. "You'd have to be living under a rock to still think that," Alabama trade industry representative Ted Kinney said.[100]

Still, many question whether these increases—or even much greater increases than have been recorded so far—can save a program that collects $2 billion in premiums each year and owes more than $20 billion to the federal government. Critics are outraged that, rather than reining in it, Congress seems to be letting wealthy people take advantage of it. An Associated Press story noted that, although the program was struggling financially after Katrina and Rita, "politicians want to extend the taxpayer-subsidized coverage for some of the riskiest—and potentially most valuable—properties in the country."[101] The article referred to a pair of laws that Congress passed in 2006 to exempt areas in Jekyll Island, Georgia, and a subdivision near Grayton Beach State Park in Florida from a 1982 federal law that denies federal benefits such as flood insurance coverage to homeowners who chose to build in coastal barrier regions that are particularly susceptible to weather disasters.

Testifying against the bills before their passage, Stephen Ellis of Taxpayers for Common Sense Action argued:

> [The Coastal Barrier Resource System] is about personal responsibility—it simply says if you want to build in harm's way, do not ask Uncle Sam to bail you out when the inevitable disaster strikes.
>
> Taxpayers for Common Sense Action has concerns about all the bills being considered at today's hearing. We have watched as the program has been nickled and dimed to death

over the years as so-called technical corrections have exposed taxpayers across the country to greater risks.[102]

Ellis made it clear that his opposition was not to building in coastal regions, but to including these high-risk developments in the National Flood Insurance Program. "They can develop and redevelop all they want, but my Uncle Sid in Omaha should not have to pay for it."[103]

With interest on its debt to the federal government eating up about a third of its revenues from insurance premiums, the NFIP stands to continue losing money for years to come, even if nothing on the order of Hurricane Katrina happens. If another Hurricane Katrina causes another shortfall surpassing $20 billion, Congress might be willing to help the program pay its policyholders, but would lawmakers be willing to continue a program operating at such a deficit?

Is Global Warming Increasing Disaster Risk?

Some have suggested that the National Flood Insurance Program should be prepared for more large-scale disasters, arguing that the 2005 hurricane season was not the "storm of the century," but rather a warning of a future in which Category 4 and Category 5 hurricanes will strike the nation with regularity. They point to global warming as the culprit.

Scientists have observed that average temperatures on Earth are rising at rate that many find alarming. The most significant organization in the study of climate change has been the Intergovernmental Panel on Climate Change (IPCC), which the United Nations and World Meteorological Organization co-founded in 1988. The group operates on a consensus model, bringing experts together to voice their opinions and develop statements in which they weigh the evidence in support of a particular position and rank the likelihood of conclusions and predictions.

In February 2007, the IPCC released a report that lent great momentum to people who are trying to combat global warming by reducing the emission of "greenhouse gases." Human activities, such as industrial production, dumping in landfills, and automobile use, have increased the concentration of gases such as carbon dioxide, methane, and nitrous oxide in the Earth's atmosphere. The consensus among scientists is that the increased concentration of these gases has led to an overall increase in the Earth's temperature; however, many continue to debate the extent to which greenhouse gas emissions should be curbed and what may be the best method to do so.

The 2007 IPCC report noted that 11 of the 12 years from 1995 to 2006 ranked among the 12 warmest years on record since global temperature tracking began in 1850. The group's scientific experts predicted that global temperatures will rise somewhere between 3.2 and 7.8 degrees Fahrenheit during the twenty-first century. Further, the report predicted that global warming would make hurricane season more dangerous: "Based on a range of models, it is likely that future tropical cyclones (typhoons and hurricanes) will become more intense, with larger peak wind speeds and more heavy precipitation associated with ongoing increases of tropical [sea surface temperatures]." Further, the report lent some credence to claims that the intensity of hurricane season already has been increasing. "The apparent increase in the proportion of very intense storms since 1970 in some regions is much larger than simulated by current models for that period," it stated.[104]

Not all scientists agree with these conclusions, however. In fact, the World Meteorological Organization had released a report only months earlier in which a panel of experts acknowledged that "global warming can cause a trend in tropical cyclone intensities," but stated that it was impossible to determine "how large a change" was occurring: "a relatively small one several decades into the future or large changes occurring today?"[105] Rather than attempting a guess, the panel stated, "This is still a hotly debated area for which we can provide no definitive conclusion."[106] Although it acknowledged that economic damages from hurricanes had skyrocketed in recent decades, the report suggested that the increase in hurricane damages "has been caused, to a large extent, by increasing coastal populations, by increasing insured values in coastal areas . . . and, perhaps, a rising sensitivity of modern societies to disruptions of infrastructure."[107]

Another effect of global warming is a rise in sea levels, as ice in the polar regions begins to melt. Sea levels already have been rising, and further increases are predicted. Ironically, FEMA issued a report in 1991 that examined the relationship between rising sea levels and the NFIP. While acknowledging that long-term increases would impact the program, and that "the region most significantly affected would be the Louisiana coast," the report concluded: "Because of the present uncertainties in the projections of potential changes in sea level and the ability of the rating system to respond easily to a 1-foot rise in sea level, there are no immediate program changes needed."[108]

Some believe that it is not necessary to answer the question of whether the increased impact of hurricanes and other disasters is the result of global warming or of population shifts. According to Evan Mills of the Lawrence Berkeley National Laboratory, "the consequences of future climate change will be amplified by economic development and the tendency of populations to move into harm's way," but it is not yet possible to determine the relative contribution of each to insurance risk.[109] Mills writes that "rising uncertainty would complicate the fundamental actuarial and pricing processes that underlie well-functioning insurance markets."[110] In other words, the combined impact of global warming and people's desire to live in coastal regions will make it very difficult for insurance companies to cover their risks.

Is Federal Disaster Insurance Feasible?

To insurance companies, the reason for the increase in economic damages caused by natural disasters is not as important as the simple fact that they are increasing—dramatically. The first

Legislative Proposals for Disaster Insurance: PDPA

Members of Congress have proposed different approaches to ensuring that consumers have access to homeowner's and renter's insurance by providing federal support for coverage of disasters such as hurricanes and earthquakes. The Policyholder Disaster Protection Act of 2007 (PDPA) takes a free-market approach, allowing insurance companies to accumulate disaster reserves without paying taxes on their earnings. An excerpt follows:

Policyholder Disaster Protection Act of 2007
The Congress makes the following findings:

(1) Rising costs resulting from natural disasters are placing an increasing strain on the ability of property and casualty insurance companies to assure payment of homeowners' claims and other insurance claims arising from major natural disasters now and in the future.

(2) Present tax laws do not provide adequate incentives to assure that natural disaster insurance is provided or, where such insurance is provided, that funds are available for payment of insurance claims in the event of future catastrophic losses from major natural disasters, as present law requires an insurer wishing to accumulate surplus assets for this purpose to do so entirely from its after-tax retained earnings.

(3) Revising the tax laws applicable to the property and casualty insurance industry to permit carefully controlled accumulation of pretax dollars in separate reserve funds devoted solely to the payment of claims arising from future major natural disasters will provide incentives for property and casualty insurers to make natural disaster insurance available, will give greater protection to the Nation's homeowners, small businesses, and other insurance consumers, and will help assure the future financial health of the Nation's insurance system as a whole.

(4) Implementing these changes will reduce the possibility that a significant portion of the private insurance system would fail in the wake of a major natural disaster and that governmental entities would be required to step in to provide relief at taxpayer expense.

Source: H.R. 164 (110th Congress).

disaster in the United States to cause $1 billion in damages took place in 1989, with Hurricane Hugo. In the 1990s, billion-dollar disasters became common, with California's Northridge earthquake causing more than $15 billion in damages and Florida's Hurricane Andrew causing $26.5 billion.

Insurance companies make money by taking on other people's risks for a price. People who face the highest level of risk pay the highest price. Therefore, people who live in areas prone to hurricanes and earthquakes pay the highest premiums for their homeowner's insurance. Because insurance is a highly regulated business, insurance companies cannot always charge people as much as they might think is necessary to cover their risk. State governments limit insurance companies' ability to raise their rates. Additionally, guessing when a disaster might occur and how much damage it might cause is extremely difficult.

The combination of price regulation and the immense costs of natural disasters has led many insurance companies to scale back or cease their operations in disaster-prone areas. In California prior to the 1994 Northridge earthquake, insurance companies were required to provide earthquake coverage. Facing more than $12 billion in claims from the earthquake, many insurance companies stopped doing business in the state. This prompted the state to start its own earthquake insurance program. In Florida, after Hurricane Andrew in 1992, losses were double what insurance companies had thought would be the "worst-case scenario" for hurricane damages. As a result, write Catherine England and Jeffrey Yousey, "The unprecedented losses from these disasters (and the fear of still higher losses from future catastrophes) have served as wake-up calls to the industry, and they have led many insurance companies to attempt to reduce their exposure to catastrophic events in states viewed as 'disaster prone.'"[111] After these disasters, insurance companies cancelled policies and stopped writing new ones.

The states, with their ability to regulate insurance companies, responded to the decreased supply of insurance available to homeowners. California established its own earthquake insurance program, using decreased financial risk to entice insurance companies back into the state insurance market. Florida took a more heavy-handed approach, limiting the number of policies that insurance companies could cancel.

These state approaches have not been entirely successful, though, and the devastation of hurricanes Katrina and Rita led to a new call for creating a federal disaster insurance program operating like the National Flood Insurance Program. Writing for the Competitive Enterprise Institute (CEI), a conservative pro-business think tank, Catherine England and Jeffrey Yousey criticized a series of 1998 proposals for federal disaster insurance. They argued that, free of government interference, the insurance industry could profitably offer disaster insurance without creating another taxpayer-subsidized program. Their proposal included three elements: first, taking away the states' power to regulate disaster insurance; second, ending federal taxation of insurance companies' cash reserve income; and third, denying federal disaster assistance to those who choose not to buy disaster assistance.

The second element, ending federal taxation of reserve income, requires further explanation. Insurance companies take the money that they collect in premiums and invest it, so that they increase the amount of money that they have available to pay claims—their reserves. The money that the insurance companies make by investing their reserves is taxed by the federal government, limiting the increase in the insurance companies' reserves and thereby reducing the amount of money available to pay when policyholders suffer losses. In *Regulation*, the Cato Institute's magazine, Scott Harrington writes: "This tax disadvantage is especially pronounced for disaster insurance because insurers must hold huge amounts of capital to pay claims that have a low probability of occurrence."[112]

Some regulators discount the free-market approach advocated by groups such as CEI and the Cato Institute. The problem, the regulators say, is that insurers operating in one state and insuring one particular type of disaster take on too much risk, while a national program would spread the risk nationwide. Noting that only about 13 percent of insured homes in California have earthquake coverage included in their policies, state insurance commissioner John Garamendi said, "The premiums for these policyholders will be extraordinarily high because the pool of risk is so small. California's propensity for disasters means that we all are at a high risk to lose our homes and other important possessions. A national policy would help spread the cost of rebuilding our lives."[113]

In 2007, Congress began debating proposals for increasing consumer access to disaster insurance, with some following a free-market approach, and others favoring government involvement in the program.

Summary

Hurricanes Katrina and Rita have shaped the debate regarding disaster assistance, not only in reference to the government's response to the 2005 hurricanes as an unprecedented event, but also as an "eye-opener," alerting the nation to the possibility that future disasters could be even more severe. Many worry that another disaster on par with Katrina could cause the demise of the National Flood Insurance Program, a possibility made more likely, some say, by global warming. With people investing heavily in disaster-prone areas, many of which consumers see as desirable places to live, some are calling for a national disaster insurance program to insure that all Americans are able to protect their investments in their homes and personal belongings.

NOTES

Introduction: When Disaster Strikes

1 Rawle O. King, *Federal Flood Insurance: The Repetitive Loss Problem*, Congressional Research Service Report for Congress RL32972 (June 30, 2005), CRS-7.

Point: The Federal Government Should Play a Stronger Role in Disaster Preparedness and Relief

2 U.S. Senate Committee on Homeland Security and Governmental Affairs, *Hurricane Katrina: A Nation Still Unprepared* (Washington, D.C., 2006), 28-4–28-5.

3 *Congressional Record* 109 (September 8, 2005): E 1801.

4 Ibid.

5 *Congressional Record* 109 (September 2, 2005): H 7629.

6 Ibid.

7 *Congressional Record* 109 (December 13, 2005): E 2515.

8 Joseph B. Treaster and Deborah Sontag, "Local Officials Criticize Federal Government Over Response," *New York Times*, September 2, 2005.

9 Kathleen Blanco, "Governor's Address," (speech, New Orleans City Council, New Orleans, LA, January 5, 2006).

10 Gene Taylor and Charlie Melancon, "Hurricane Katrina: Recommendations for Legislative Action" [.pdf], http://www.house.gov/genetaylor/KTF .Katrina&Beyond.PBFormat.pdf.

11 Ibid.

12 Ibid.

13 Testimony of Governor Kathleen Blanco speaking before the Subcommittee on Water Resources and Environment and the Subcommittee on Economic Development, Public Buildings, and Emergency Management Committee on Transportation and Infrastructure, October 18, 2005.

14 Taylor and Melancon, p. 5.

15 U.S. Senate Committee, *A Nation Still Unprepared*, Recommendation 55, p. 625.

16 Kathleen Blanco, "Back to Business," October 6, 2005, http://gov.louisiana .gov/index.cfm?md=newsroom&tmp=de tail&catID=4&articleID=854&navID=13.

Counterpoint: Local and State Governments Should Accept More Responsibility for Disaster Preparedness and Relief

17 Ray Nagin, interview by WWL Radio, September 1, 2005. http://edition.cnn .com/2005/US/09/02/nagin.transcript/ index.html.

18 Brian DeBose, "Blacks Fault Lack of Local Leadership," *Washington Times*, September 10, 2005.

19 Russell S. Sobel and Peter T. Leeson, *Flirting with Disaster: The Inherent Problems with FEMA*, Policy Brief no. 573 (Washington, D.C.: Cato Institute, July 19, 2006).

20 Cato Institute, "Did Big Government Return with Katrina?" *Cato Policy Report* (Nov./Dec. 2005), p. 4.

21 Americans for Tax Reform, "Policy Brief: The Facts about Federal Spending" (Washington, D.C., Feb. 13, 2006).

22 Bureau of Labor Statistics, *Career Guide to Industries* (Washington, D.C., 2006), p. 272.

23 Sobel and Leeson, *Flirting with Disaster*, 2.

24 Ibid., pp. 5–6.

25 Ibid., p. 6.

26 Institute Task Force, *Empowering America: A Proposal for Enhancing Regional Preparedness*, Heritage Special Report (April 7, 2006), p. 2.

27 Rick Perry, "Federalizing Disaster Response" (Heritage Foundation Lecture No. 905, Washington, D.C., November 7, 2005).

28 Senate Committee, *A Nation Still Unprepared*, Conclusions, p. 586.

29 Ibid.

30 Ibid., Findings-21.

31 Governor's Commission on Recovery, Rebuilding, and Renewal, *After Katrina: Building Back Better Than Ever* (Jackson, Miss., 2005), p. v.

32 Haley Barbour, "State of the State

Address" (speech, Jackson, MS, January 9, 2006).

33 Ibid.

34 Ibid.

35 Ibid.

36 Governor's Commission, *After Katrina*, p. vi.

37 Ibid., p. 2.

Point: Federal Financial Assistance to Disaster Victims Is Inadequate

38 Associated Press, "Brown: Party politics played role in Katrina response," January 20, 2007. http://www.cnn.com/2007/POLITICS/01/20/katrina.brown.ap/index.html.

39 Kathleen B. Blanco. "Fighting for Louisiana's Fair Share" [speech], January 23, 2007. Office of the Governor. http://www.gov.state.la.us/index.cfm?md=newsroom&tmp=detail&catID=4&articleID=2533&navID=13.

40 Kathleen Blanco, Letter to Nancy Pelosi. Jan. 23, 2007.

41 Susan J. Popkin, Margery A. Turner, and Martha Burt, *Rebuilding Affordable Housing in New Orleans: The Challenge of Creating Inclusive Communities* (Washington, D.C.: Urban Institute, 2006), p. 2.

42 Ibid.

43 Tracie L. Washington, Brian D. Smedley, Beatrice Alvarez, and Jason Reece, *Housing in New Orleans: One Year After Katrina* (Baltimore, Md.: NAACP, 2006), p. 23.

44 Rudolph G. Penner, *Insuring Against Catastrophes: The Lessons from Katrina* (Washington, D.C.: Urban Institute, 2006), p. 7.

45 FEMA press release, "FEMA Expedited Assistance Continues Flowing," September 9, 2005.

46 *Congressional Record* 109 (September 13, 2005): S 9952–9953.

47 Amy Liu, "A Review of the Federal Response to Rebuilding Mississippi: One Year after Hurricane Katrina," in *Envisioning a Better Mississippi: Hurricane*

Katrina and Mississippi: One Year Later (Jackson: Mississippi NAACP, 2006), p. 9.

48 Letter from Shelia Crowley to Michael Chertoff, Alphonso Jackson, and R. David Paulison (October 17, 2006).

49 Liu, "A Review of the Federal Response," p. 12.

50 Washington et al., *Housing in New Orleans*, p. 25.

51 Olivia Golden, *Young Children after Katrina: A Proposal to Heal the Damage and Create Opportunity in New Orleans* (Washington, D.C.: Urban Institute, 2006), p. 2.

52 Ibid., pp. 8–9.

53 Blanco, "Back to Business."

Counterpoint: Federal Financial Assistance to Disaster Victims Is Wasteful

54 U.S. Department of Justice press release, "Alabama Woman Sentenced to More than Six Years in Prison for Katrina Fraud," January 24, 2007.

55 U.S. Government Accountability Office, *Hurricanes Katrina and Rita Disaster Relief: Continued Findings of Fraud, Waste, and Abuse*, GAO-07-252T (December 6, 2006), p. 14.

56 Scott E. Harrington, "Rethinking Disaster Policy," *Regulation* 23, no. 1 (2003), p. 44.

57 Michelle Malkin, "Quake Relief: Will Handouts Haunt Us?" *Insight on the News*, March 14, 1994, Retrieved January 26, 2007 from looksmart.com database.

58 Wharton School of the University of Pennsylvania, "Hurricane Katrina: Important Policy Questions Amid the Devastation and Recovery," *Knowledge@Wharton* (January 25, 2206), p. 3.

59 Joanne Linnerooth-Bayer, Reinhard Mechler, and Georg Pflug, "Refocusing Disaster Aid," *Science* 309 (2005), p. 1046.

60 Government Accountability Office, *Hurricanes Katrina and Rita Disaster Relief: Improper and Potentially Fraudulent Individual Assistance Payments Estimated*

to Be Between $600 Million and $1.4 Billion, GAO-06-844T (June 14, 2006).

61 GAO, *Hurricanes Katrina and Rita Disaster Relief: Continued Findings*, p. 9.

62 Ibid.

63 Malkin, "Quake Relief: Will Handouts Haunt Us?"

64 Ibid.

65 GAO, *Hurricanes Katrina and Rita Disaster Relief: Continued Findings*, p. 6.

Point: The National Flood Insurance Program Must Be Maintained or Expanded

66 Chad Berginnis, testifying before the Senate Committee on Banking, Housing, and Urban Affairs, on the future of the National Flood Insurance Program, October 18, 2005, p. xx.

67 Anthony S. Lowe, testifying before the Senate Subcommittee on Economic Policy, Committee on Banking, Housing, and Urban Affairs, on National Flood Insurance repetitive losses, March 25, 2004.

68 Rawle O. King, *National Flood Insurance Program: Treasury Borrowing in the Aftermath of Hurricane Katrina*, Congressional Research Service Report for Congress RS22394 (June 6, 2006).

69 Berginnis testimony, October 18, 2005.

70 Steven Feldmann, testifying before the Senate Subcommittee on Economic Policy, Committee on Banking, Housing, and Urban Affairs, on National Flood Insurance repetitive losses, March 25, 2004.

71 Ibid.

72 Ibid.

73 Ibid.

74 Lloyd Dixon, Noreen Clancy, Seth A. Seabury, and Adrian Overton, *The National Flood Insurance Program's Market Penetration Rate: Estimates and Policy Implications* (Santa Monica, CA: RAND Corporation, 2006).

75 Pamela Mayer Pogue, testifying before the Senate Committee on Banking, Housing, and Urban Affairs, on the National Flood Insurance Program, February 2, 2006.

76 Ibid.

77 Berginnis testimony, October 18, 2005.

78 19 Stat. 1570 (1936). Cited in Nicole T. Carter, *Flood Risk Management: Federal Role in Infrastructure*, Congressional Research Service Report for Congress RL33129 (Oct. 26, 2005), p CRS-2.

79 King, *The Repetitive Loss Problem*, CRS-2.

80 Regina M. Lowrie, testifying before the Senate Committee on Banking, Housing, and Urban Affairs, on the National Flood Insurance Program, February 2, 2006.

Counterpoint: The National Flood Insurance Program Must Be Reformed or Eliminated

81 John Stossel, "Confessions of a Welfare Queen," *Reason* (March 2004). http://www.reason.com/news/show/29067.html.

82 Ibid.

83 Donald B. Marron, testifying before the Senate Committee on Banking, Housing, and Urban Affairs, on the National Flood Insurance Program, January 25, 2006.

84 David C. John, testifying before the Senate Committee on Banking, Housing, and Urban Affairs, on the National Flood Insurance Program, February 2, 2006.

85 Ibid.

86 Carolyn Dehring, "The Value of Building Codes," *Regulation* (Summer 2006), p. 13.

87 Harrington, "Rethinking Disaster Policy," p. 44.

88 Paul J. Gessing, testifying before the Senate Committee on Banking, Housing, and Urban Affairs, on the National Flood Insurance Program, February 2, 2006.

89 Dehring, "The Value of Building Codes," p. 13.

90 John testimony, February 2, 2006.

91 Hunter testimony, February 2, 2006.

92 Ibid.

93 John testimony, February 2, 2006.

94 J. Robert Hunter, testimony before the Senate Committee on Banking, Housing, and Urban Affairs, on the National Flood Insurance Program, February 2, 2006.

95 Fireman's Fund press release, "Fireman's Fund Announces Surface Water and Flood Coverage," June 7, 2006.

96 Gessing testimony, February 2, 2006.

97 Hunter testimony, February 2, 2006.

Conclusion: Future Directions in Disaster Relief

98 FEMA press release, "Enough Disaster Assistance For All," August 21, 2006.

99 Ibid.

100 Ben Evans, "Sales of Federal Flood Insurance Policies Rose 13% in 2006," *Insurance Journal* (January 8, 2007).

101 Associated Press, "Katrina Home Owners Stress Federal Flood Insurance Program," December 29, 2006.

102 Stephen Ellis, testifying before the House Subcommittee on Fisheries and Oceans, Resource Committee, Legislative Hearing on HR 138, HR 479, HR 1656, HR 3280 and HR 4165, April 6, 2006.

103 Ibid.

104 Intergovernmental Panel on Climate Change, *Climate Change 2007: The Physical Science Basis, Summary for Policymakers* (Geneva, Switzerland, 2007), p. 12.

105 World Meteorological Organization, *Statement on Tropical Cyclones and Climate Change* (Geneva, Switzerland, 2006), p. 4.

106 Ibid.

107 Ibid., p. 7.

108 Federal Insurance Administration, FEMA, *Projected Impact of Relative Sea Level Rise on the National Flood Insurance Program* (Washington, D.C., 1991): p. ii.

109 Evan Mills, "Insurance in a Climate of Change," *Science* 309 (2005): 1042.

110 Ibid.

111 Catherine England and Jeffrey R. Yousey, *Insuring Against Natural Disasters: Possibilities for Market-Based Reform* (Washington, D.C.: Competitive Enterprise Institute, 1998), p. 2.

112 Scott E. Harrington, "Rethinking Disaster Policy," *Regulation* 23, no. 1 (2003), p. 42.

113 California Department of Insurance press release, "State Insurance Commissioner John Garamendi Proposes Creation of National 'Natural Disaster Insurance Program,'" October 6, 2004.

Books and Reports

Comerio, Mary C. *Disaster Hits Home: New Policy for Urban Housing Recovery.* Berkeley: University of California Press, 1998.

Daniels, Ronald J., Donald F. Kettl, and Howard Kunreuther, eds. *On Risk and Disaster: Lessons from Hurricane Katrina.* Philadelphia: University of Pennsylvania Press, 2006.

Governor's Commission on Recovery, Rebuilding, and Renewal. *After Katrina: Building Back Better Than Ever.* Jackson, Miss., 2005.

Kunreuther, Howard, and Richard Roth, Sr., eds. *The Status and Role of Insurance against Natural Disasters in the United States.* Washington, D.C.: Joseph Henry Press, 1998.

Lindel, Michael K., and Ronald W. Perry, eds. *Communicating Environmental Risk in Multiethnic Communities.* Thousand Oaks, Calif.: Sage Publications, 2003.

Platt, Rutherford H., ed. *Disasters and Democracy: The Politics of Extreme Natural Events.* Washington, D.C.: Island Press, 1999.

U.S. Senate Committee on Homeland Security and Governmental Affairs. *Hurricane Katrina: A Nation Still Unprepared.* Washington, D.C.: U.S. Government Printing Office, 2006.

Washington, Tracie L., Brian D. Smedley, Beatrice Alvarez, and Jason Reece. *Housing in New Orleans: One Year After Katrina.* Baltimore, Md.: NAACP, 2006.

White House. *The Federal Response to Katrina: Lessons Learned.* Washington, D.C., U.S. Government Printing Office, 2006.

Web Sites

ACORN

www.acorn.org
ACORN is a national alliance of groups representing low-income families. It advocates for assistance for low-income people affected by disasters such as hurricanes Katrina and Rita.

Association of State Floodplain Managers

www.floods.org
This is an organization of officials involved in administering flood insurance, making floodplains safer, and otherwise protecting people from flood damage. It provides insight into a number of policy issues related to flooding.

Cato Institute

www.cato.org
This libertarian think tank supports individual responsibility and limited government. It opposes use of taxpayer money for disaster relief and government support of insurance programs.

Competitive Enterprise Institute

www.cei.org
The CEI ia a conservative pro-business think tank generally opposing government involvement in disaster relief and disaster insurance.

Consumer Federation of America

www.consumerfed.org
National alliance of pro-consumer organizations, advocating on behalf of consumers on a number of issues, including insurance issues. The group's director of insurance is the former director of the National Flood Insurance Program.

Federal Emergency Management Agency

www.fema.gov
This federal agency is primarily responsible for federal disaster assistance. Provides information on preparing for and recovering from disasters.

Intergovernmental Program on Climate Change

www.ipcc.ch
This United Nations–sponsored panel of scientific experts studies global warming, including the effects of global warming on hurricanes and other disasters.

National Association for the Advancement of Colored People

www.naacp.org
This civil rights organization is deeply concerned about disaster relief and recovery efforts due to the disproportionate impact that some disasters—notably Hurricane Katrina—have had on African Americans.

National Flood Insurance Program

www.floodsmart.gov
Information for homeowners, the public, and journalists about the flood insurance program, how it operates, its benefits, and the risks of going without flood insurance.

New Orleans Times-Picayune Katrina Archives

www.nola.com/katrina
Extensive collection of newspaper articles about Hurricane Katrina, including first-hand accounts from those left behind during the evacuation of New Orleans.

Urban Institute

www.urban.org
This organization conducts research and policy analysis on issues affecting U.S. cities. Produced a series of reports on Katrina recovery efforts, focusing in particular on the impact on New Orleans.

Cases and Statutes

Flood Insurance Reform Act of 2004, Pub. Law No. 108-264.
Law intended to reduce financial losses by the National Flood Insurance Program by allowing the program to buy or renovate properties on which multiple insurance claims have been made.

In re Katrina Levee Breaches Consolidated Litigation, No. 05-4182 (E.D. La., Nov. 27, 2006).
Federal ruling that policies excluding flood damage did not explicitly include damage caused by the failure of New Orleans' levees during Hurricane Katrina.

National Flood Insurance Act, 42 U.S. Code, Sec. 4001.
Law establishing the National Flood Insurance Program to ensure the availability of affordable coverage to the American public.

Robert T. Stafford Disaster Relief and Emergency Assistance Act ("Stafford Act"), 42 U.S. Code, Chap. 68.
Comprehensive law governing federal disaster relief efforts, including emergency preparedness, declaration of a disaster, and disaster relief. The law also outlines state responsibilities in cases of disaster.

Terms and Concepts

actuarial rates

big government

efficiency

enumerated powers

federalism

global warming

greenhouse gases

mitigation

moral hazard

mortgage

police powers

reinsurance

risk-sharing

risk management

subsidies

119

APPENDIX

Beginning Legal Research

The goal of POINT/COUNTERPOINT is not only to provide the reader with an introduction to a controversial issue affecting society, but also to encourage the reader to explore the issue more fully. This appendix, then, is meant to serve as a guide to the reader in researching the current state of the law as well as exploring some of the public-policy arguments as to why existing laws should be changed or new laws are needed.

Like many types of research, legal research has become much faster and more accessible with the invention of the Internet. This appendix discusses some of the best starting points, but of course "surfing the Net" will uncover endless additional sources of information—some more reliable than others. Some important sources of law are not yet available on the Internet, but these can generally be found at the larger public and university libraries. Librarians usually are happy to point patrons in the right direction.

The most important source of law in the United States is the Constitution. Originally enacted in 1787, the Constitution outlines the structure of our federal government and sets limits on the types of laws that the federal government and state governments can pass. Through the centuries, a number of amendments have been added to or changed in the Constitution, most notably the first ten amendments, known collectively as the Bill of Rights, which guarantee important civil liberties. Each state also has its own constitution, many of which are similar to the U.S. Constitution. It is important to be familiar with the U.S. Constitution because so many of our laws are affected by its requirements. State constitutions often provide protections of individual rights that are even stronger than those set forth in the U.S. Constitution.

Within the guidelines of the U.S. Constitution, Congress—both the House of Representatives and the Senate—passes bills that are either vetoed or signed into law by the president. After the passage of the law, it becomes part of the United States Code, which is the official compilation of federal laws. The state legislatures use a similar process, in which bills become law when signed by the state's governor. Each state has its own official set of laws, some of which are published by the state and some of which are published by commercial publishers. The U.S. Code and the state codes are an important source of legal research; generally, legislators make efforts to make the language of the law as clear as possible.

However, reading the text of a federal or state law generally provides only part of the picture. In the American system of government, after the

legislature passes laws and the executive (U.S. president or state governor) signs them, it is up to the judicial branch of the government, the court system, to interpret the laws and decide whether they violate any provision of the Constitution. At the state level, each state's supreme court has the ultimate authority in determining what a law means and whether or not it violates the state constitution. However, the federal courts—headed by the U.S. Supreme Court—can review state laws and court decisions to determine whether they violate federal laws or the U.S. Constitution. For example, a state court may find that a particular criminal law is valid under the state's constitution, but a federal court may then review the state court's decision and determine that the law is invalid under the U.S. Constitution.

It is important, then, to read court decisions when doing legal research. The Constitution uses language that is intentionally very general—for example, prohibiting "unreasonable searches and seizures" by the police—and court cases often provide more guidance. For example, the U.S. Supreme Court's 2001 decision in *Kyllo* v. *United States* held that scanning the outside of a person's house using a heat sensor to determine whether the person is growing marijuana is unreasonable—*if* it is done without a search warrant secured from a judge. Supreme Court decisions provide the most definitive explanation of the law of the land, and it is therefore important to include these in research. Often, when the Supreme Court has not decided a case on a particular issue, a decision by a federal appeals court or a state supreme court can provide guidance; but just as laws and constitutions can vary from state to state, so can federal courts be split on a particular interpretation of federal law or the U.S. Constitution. For example, federal appeals courts in Louisiana and California may reach opposite conclusions in similar cases.

Lawyers and courts refer to statutes and court decisions through a formal system of citations. Use of these citations reveals which court made the decision (or which legislature passed the statute) and when and enables the reader to locate the statute or court case quickly in a law library. For example, the legendary Supreme Court case *Brown* v. *Board of Education* has the legal citation 347 U.S. 483 (1954). At a law library, this 1954 decision can be found on page 483 of volume 347 of the U.S. Reports, the official collection of the Supreme Court's decisions. Citations can also be helpful in locating court cases on the Internet.

Understanding the current state of the law leads only to a partial understanding of the issues covered by the POINT/COUNTERPOINT series. For a fuller understanding of the issues, it is necessary to look at public-policy arguments that the current state of the law is not adequately addressing the issue.

Many groups lobby for new legislation or changes to existing legislation; the National Rifle Association (NRA), for example, lobbies Congress and the state legislatures constantly to make existing gun control laws less restrictive and not to pass additional laws. The NRA and other groups dedicated to various causes might also intervene in pending court cases: a group such as Planned Parenthood might file a brief *amicus curiae* (as "a friend of the court")—called an "amicus brief"—in a lawsuit that could affect abortion rights. Interest groups also use the media to influence public opinion, issuing press releases and frequently appearing in interviews on news programs and talk shows. The books in POINT/COUNTERPOINT list some of the interest groups that are active in the issue at hand, but in each case there are countless other groups working at the local, state, and national levels. It is important to read everything with a critical eye, for sometimes interest groups present information in a way that can be read only to their advantage. The informed reader must always look for bias.

Finding sources of legal information on the Internet is relatively simple thanks to "portal" sites such as FindLaw (*www.findlaw.com*), which provides access to a variety of constitutions, statutes, court opinions, law review articles, news articles, and other resources—including all Supreme Court decisions issued since 1893. Other useful sources of information include the U.S. Government Printing Office (*www.gpo.gov*), which contains a complete copy of the U.S. Code, and the Library of Congress's THOMAS system (*thomas.loc.gov*), which offers access to bills pending before Congress as well as recently passed laws. Of course, the Internet changes every second of every day, so it is best to do some independent searching. Most cases, studies, and opinions that are cited or referred to in public debate can be found online—and *everything* can be found in one library or another.

The Internet can provide a basic understanding of most important legal issues, but not all sources can be found there. To find some documents it is necessary to visit the law library of a university or a public law library; some cities have public law libraries, and many library systems keep legal documents at the main branch. On the following page are some common citation forms.

COMMON CITATION FORMS

Source of Law	Sample Citation	Notes
U.S. Supreme Court	*Employment Division v. Smith*, 485 U.S. 660 (1988)	The U.S. Reports is the official record of Supreme Court decisions. There is also an unofficial Supreme Court ("S. Ct.") reporter.
U.S. Court of Appeals	*United States v. Lambert*, 695 F.2d 536 (11th Cir.1983)	Appellate cases appear in the Federal Reporter, designated by "F." The 11th Circuit has jurisdiction in Alabama, Florida, and Georgia.
U.S. District Court	*Carillon Importers, Ltd. v. Frank Pesce Group, Inc.*, 913 F.Supp. 1559 (S.D.Fla.1996)	Federal trial-level decisions are reported in the Federal Supplement ("F. Supp."). Some states have multiple federal districts; this case originated in the Southern District of Florida.
U.S. Code	Thomas Jefferson Commemoration Commission Act, 36 U.S.C., §149 (2002)	Sometimes the popular names of legislation—names with which the public may be familiar—are included with the U.S. Code citation.
State Supreme Court	*Sterling v. Cupp*, 290 Ore. 611, 614, 625 P.2d 123, 126 (1981)	The Oregon Supreme Court decision is reported in both the state's reporter and the Pacific regional reporter.
State Statute	Pennsylvania Abortion Control Act of 1982, 18 Pa. Cons. Stat. 3203-3220 (1990)	States use many different citation formats for their statutes.

CONTRIBUTOR ///////

ALAN MARZILLI, M.A., J.D., lives in Washington, D.C., and is a program associate with Advocates for Human Potential, Inc., a research and consulting firm based in Sudbury, Mass., and Albany, N.Y. He works primarily on developing training and educational materials for agencies of the federal government on topics such as housing, mental health policy, employment, and transportation. He has spoken on mental health issues in 30 states, the District of Columbia, and Puerto Rico; his work has included training mental health administrators, nonprofit management and staff, and people with mental illnesses and their families on a wide variety of topics, including effective advocacy, community-based mental health services, and housing. Marzilli has written several handbooks and training curricula that are used nationally and as far away as the U.S. territory of Guam. Additionally, he managed statewide and national mental health advocacy programs and worked for several public interest lobbying organizations while studying law at Georgetown University. Marzilli has written more than a dozen books, including numerous titles in the POINT/COUNTERPOINT series.

PICTURE CREDITS ///////